Conservation in London

A study of strategic planning policy in London

ENGLISH HERITAGE

LONDON PLANNING ADVISORY COMMITTEE

LPAC
LONDON PLANNING
ADVISORY COMMITTEE

1995

First published 1995 by English Heritage, 23 Savile Row, London W1X
1AB

Printed by Quadrant Offset

A catalogue record for this book is available from the British Library

Edited by Kate Macdonald
Designed by Nick Cannan

ISBN 1 85074 522 6

A   don

Contents

Acknowledgements

English Heritage and the London Planning Advisory Committee (LPAC) gratefully acknowledge the time, assistance, and contributions made to this study by these individuals and organisations: Nick Antram (London Borough of Tower Hamlets), Jane Carlson (LPAC), Michael Coupe (English Heritage), Chris Donovan (London Borough of Bexley), James Edgar (English Heritage), Jon Finney (London Borough of Hillingdon), Steve Gould (London Borough of Haringey), Graham King (City of Westminster), Andrew Lainton (London Borough of Brent), Aidan McDowell (Department of National Heritage), Clare Parfitt (English Heritage), Jenny Pearce (London Borough of Richmond), Neil Whitehead (Government Office for London), and Kate Williamson (City of London).

Publication of this study does not necessarily indicate that its views and recommendations are accepted by English Heritage and LPAC. The sponsors cannot be responsible for any loss or damage, however sustained, by others arising from reliance on the contents of this study.

Except where credited otherwise all photographs are by the English Heritage Photographic Studio.

Philip Davies, English Heritage
Robin Clement, LPAC
Joint Project Directors
January 1995

List of figures

List of tables

1 Introduction

This report on London's historic environment is based on a study by Land Use Consultants, in association with Drivers Jonas and Conservation Architecture and Planning, and on work by Andrew Saint of English Heritage, between March and July 1994. It was commissioned jointly by English Heritage and the London Planning Advisory Committee (LPAC) to provide supporting information for the preparation of supplementary advice to the Secretary of State for the Environment on strategic planning in London.

These recommendations are also directed at all those with an interest in conservation in the capital. These range from Government departments, such as National Heritage, Transport, and the Government Office for London, to those actively involved in environmental management at local level, including the London Boroughs and local conservation groups and amenity societies.

Background

While recognising the considerable achievements of conservation policy and practice in London, both English Heritage and LPAC are concerned that the city's historic environment, one of its most precious assets, continues to be under threat from inappropriate development and other adverse change. They believe that this has serious implications, not least in detracting from the achievement of LPAC's four-fold vision for London: a strong economy, a good quality of life, a sustainable future, and opportunities for all.

These concerns were most recently expressed in *Issues and Choices* (LPAC 1992a) and at a symposium, staged in July 1993 by Vision for London, on the future of conservation in London. Vision for London provides an information exchange and a forum for discussion on issues concerned with the sustainability of London and the quality of life within it. The symposium brought together many experienced people and professionals from the public, private, and voluntary sectors concerned with London's historic environment.

One of the issues which emerged from the day was the need for more effective strategic planning policies to conserve and enhance London's historic environment, taking into account LPAC's advice to the Secretary of State. As a result, English Heritage and LPAC commissioned the study on which this report is based.

Aim and objectives

The aim of this report is to define strategic planning policy options for 1996 to 2010, seeking to integrate the conservation, enhancement, and positive use of London's historic environment with evolving patterns of regeneration and development in the capital. There were five main objectives:

• to define the extent of London's historic environment on a map

• to identify the main land-use and other trends which have led to change in London's historic environment (either deterioration or enhancement), and, if possible, to plot geographical areas where these have been most significant

• to identify and plot land-use and other changes which are likely to affect London's historic environment (eg major infrastructure projects and development proposals) in 1996 to 2010

• to assess the economic and social value (both positive and negative) of London's historic environment and to ensure that this is fully reflected in strategic planning policy options in the study

• to make recommendations to the relevant Secretaries of State and other agencies on conservation policy in London

Main tasks

This report is made up of four main parts.

A description of London's historic environment

The description of London's historic environment consists of two elements. The first is an attempt to quantify the extent of the historic environment represented by statutory designations and non-statutory definitions. A designation defined by statute, such as a conservation area, differs from a non-statutory definition which refers to an area defined by policy but not covered by specific legislation. An example of the latter is an Area of Special Character, first defined in the Greater London Development Plan (GLDP).

The data for defining the historic environment was obtained from Unitary Development Plans (UDPs) and other supporting material collated by the London Boroughs. However, a telephone survey of the 33 London boroughs was carried out to collect additional information on locally-listed buildings, parks and gardens, London Squares, strategic and local views, and Areas of Special Character. This map-based information was used to generate a digitised map of the historic environment.

The second element of the description is based on work by Andrew Saint of English Heritage, and considers the evolution of London, highlighting the features which make it unique.

The value of conservation in London

Three aspects of the value of conservation were researched; environmental, social, and economic. The environmental and social aspects were assessed by looking at existing research. The economic aspects were also examined, supplemented by additional case study research on the effect on residential property values of conservation policies (listed buildings and conservation areas) and the role of conservation in urban regeneration.

The effects of land-use trends on the historic environment

The main land-use trends which led to a deterioration or improvement in London's historic environment were identified by statistical and other research material compiled by a number of organisations. Guidance on likely future trends came from similar sources, supplemented by information about development scenarios in planning policy documents.

The policy context for conservation

The fourth part of this report establishes the coverage of conservation in planning policy and guidance formulated internationally and by the UK Government.

Contents of the report

Chapter 2 describes the unique character and quality of London's historic environment. This is supported by a 'map of the historic environment' and a quantitative analysis of the planning designations and definitions which reflect it. Chapter 3 demonstrates the value of London's historic environment from environmental, economic, and social perspectives. Chapter 4 describes the main land-use changes in recent years, their recent effects on the historic environment, and some of the main changes that are likely to occur by 2010. Chapter 5 outlines the policy context in which strategic guidance on the conservation of London's historic environment must be considered. It considers policy and guidance formulated both internationally in Europe, and by Europe and the UK Government. The final chapter sets out the conclusions of the report and its recommendations on how to ensure that conservation, enhancement, and the positive use of the historic environment is a central concern in the future strategic planning of London. It also suggests which agencies should take a lead role in implementation.

2 The historic environment

London is one of the most important historic cities in the world. Understanding the general characteristics that make its fabric and environment so important is the key to identifying what we should be aiming to safeguard and enhance. This chapter provides such an understanding in two ways.

The first is an attempt to quantify the historic environment based on planning designations and definitions which exist to conserve and enhance areas, buildings, and features of historic interest. The second is to record the views of an historian, a more qualitative interpretation of the evolution of London. Together they combine to make a picture of the nature and extent of London's historic resource.

Planning designations and definitions

It could be argued that almost all of London is 'historic', and clearly some areas and features are of more value than others. This historic resource is reflected by planning designations and definitions.

Designations
Listed buildings
World Heritage Sites
Scheduled Ancient Monuments
Conservation Areas
London Squares

Definitions
Areas of Archaeological Priority/Significance
Areas of Special Character
Heritage Land
Historic Parks and Gardens
Strategic and Local Views

The area-based designations and definitions are presented as maps (see Fig 1 and Appendix 1). The mapped elements of the historic environment are a combination of nationally recognised designations and definitions of historic interest, eg Conservation Areas and Areas of Archaeological Priority, and definitions of land considered to be of London-wide interest, eg Heritage Land and Areas of

Fig 1 Composite map of the historic environment

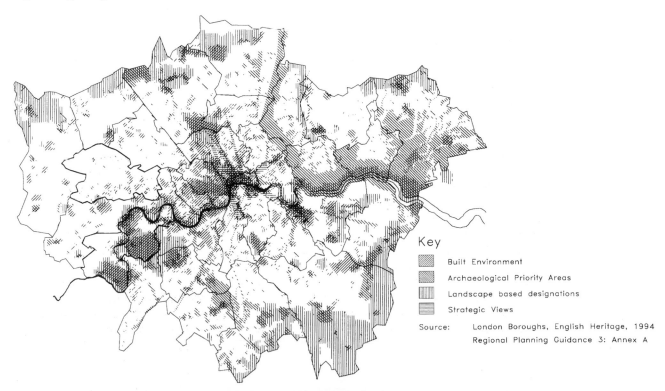

Key

▨ Built Environment
▧ Archaeological Priority Areas
▥ Landscape based designations
▤ Strategic Views

Source: London Boroughs, English Heritage, 1994
          Regional Planning Guidance 3: Annex A

Table 1 Distribution of listed buildings

	listed buildings	listed buildings as % of Greater London total	grade I/A	grade II★/B	grade II/C
Barking & Dagenham	28	0.1	3	3	22
Barnet	551	1.6	2	57	492
Bexley	123	0.4	6	8	109
Brent	175	0.5	1	6	168
Bromley	375	1.1	8	9	358
Camden	3890	11.1	255	272	3363
City	590	1.7	84	61	445
Croydon	149	0.4	6	8	135
Ealing	385	1.1	6	15	364
Enfield	378	1.1	3	20	355
Greenwich	879	2.5	41	63	775
Hackney	1130	3.2	8	36	1086
Hammersmith & Fulham	434	1.2	1	15	418
Haringey	336	1.0	4	26	306
Harrow	302	0.9	4	18	280
Havering	171	0.5	6	14	151
Hillingdon	441	1.3	6	21	414
Hounslow	602	1.7	31	23	548
Islington	4000*	8.5**	13**	25**	2937**
Kensington & Chelsea	3740	10.7	12	237	3491
Kingston	156	0.5	3	10	143
Lambeth	2063	5.9	6	56	2001
Lewisham	446	1.3	2	24	420
Merton	293	0.8	3	8	282
Newham	113	0.3	4	4	105
Redbridge	129	0.4	1	10	118
Richmond	988	2.8	46	93	849
Southwark	1403	4.0	4	18	1381
Sutton	217	0.6	1	11	205
Tower Hamlets	1892	5.4	30	34	1828
Waltham Forest	100	0.3	0	11	89
Wandsworth	352	1.0	4	22	326
Westminster	9247	26.4	375	594	8278
Total	35053		979	1832	32242

Figures refer to number of entries rather than buildings and were correct as of August 1994. An updated list for Islington was published in October 1994 showing an increase in the total number of listed buildings in the Borough to approximately 4,000. Source: English Heritage, 1994
*Approximate figure based on recent survey **Based on earlier figures

Special Character, layered to produce a composite map. Elements not included in the map are generally point sources, notably listed buildings, scheduled ancient monuments, and World Heritage Sites. The distribution of listed buildings is shown in Table 1. Information from the Boroughs determined the nature and extent of coverage of local designations and definitions (see Table 2). A commentary on the geographic distribution of the built environment, landscape and open space,

Table 2 Results of the survey of London Boroughs

Borough	LLB	no (4*)	IPG	LS	no	SV	LV pol	LV sp	LASC criteria for designation
Barking & Dagenham	2*	23	✗	✗	-	✓	1*	1*	-
Barnet	✓	644	✗	✗	-	✗	✗	✗	-
Bexley	✓	220	✗	✗	-	✗	✓	✗	residential quality
Brent	✓	(60)	1*	✗	-	✗	✓	✓	residential quality
Bromley	✓	(510)	✗	✗	-	✗	✓	✓	landscape & residential
Camden	✗	-	✗	✓	57	✓	✓	✗	-
Croydon	✓	700	✗	✗	-	✓	✗	✗	C A type
Ealing	✓	300	✗	✗	-	✗	✓	✓	C A type
Enfield	✓	(113)	✗	✗	-	✗	✓	✓	landscape
Greenwich	✓	1720	✗	✗	-	✓	✓	✓	C A type & landscape
Hackney	✓	1200	✗	✓	13	✓	✗	✗	landscape
Hammersmith & Fulham	✓	(1500)	✗	✗	-	✓	✗	✗	-
Haringey	✓	200	✗	✗	-	✓	✓	✓	-
Harrow	✓	(350)	✗	✗	-	✗	✓	✗	-
Havering	✗	-	✗	✗	-	✗	✗	✗	-
Hillingdon	✓	125	✗	✗	-	✗	✓	✗	C A type
Hounslow	✓	(54)	✗	✗	-	✗	✗	✗	-
Islington	✓	5000	✗	✓	μ	✓	✓	✓	C A type
Kensington & Chelsea	✗	-	✗	✓	80	✓	✓	5*	use/landscape/heritage
Kingston	✓	(500)	✗	✗	-	✗	✓	✓	C A type
Lambeth	✗	-	✗	✓	22	✓	✓	✓	-
Lewisham	✓	190	✗	✓	13	✓	✓	✓	landscape
Merton	3*	-	✗	✗	-	✗	✗	✗	-
Newham	✓	133	✗	✗	-	✗	✗	✗	C A type
Redbridge	✓	(100)	✗	✗	-	✗	✗	✗	residential quality
Richmond	✓	1800	✗	✗	-	✓	✓	✓	-
Southwark	✓	500	✗	✗	-	✓	✓	✗	-
Sutton	3*	-	✗	✗	-	✗	✗	✗	C A type
Tower Hamlets	✓	700	✗	✓	16	✓	✓	✓	-
Waltham Forest	✓	(84)	1*	✗	-	✗	✗	✗	-
Wandsworth	✓	1000	✗	✗	-	✓	✓	✓	-
Westminster	✗	-	✗	✓	μ	✓	✓	✗	-
City of London	✗	-	✗	✗	-	✓	✓	✓	-

Key
LLB = locally listed building
IPG = inventory of parks and gardens
LS = London squares
SV = strategic views
LV = local views
  pol = general policy
  sp = specific views identified
LASC = locally designated area of special character
CA = conservation area
no = number

1* = considering taking on designation
2* = currently a proposal
3* = under preparation
4* = figures in brackets relate to approximate number of entries on list.
     Each entry may include a number of buildings.
5* = although not referred to in UDP, aware of specific views used in
     non-statutory documents.
μ = number unknown

Source: London Boroughs, 1994

Fig 2 No 3 King's Bench Walk, Inner Temple (Photo Greater London Record Office Photograph Collection)

views, and archaeology of London's historic environment is below. Relevant background information on designations and definitions is given in Appendix 1.

The built environment

London possesses an immensely rich built fabric of considerable historic interest. This is reflected in the high incidence of designations and definitions for its protection. It includes two of Britain's ten World Heritage Sites, the Palace of Westminster/Westminster Abbey and the Tower of London. In addition, there are some 800 Conservation Areas in Greater London, covering 25% of the area of the capital. This amounts to 10% of the total of Conservation Areas in England and Wales and compares with 32 Conservation Areas in Edinburgh and 29 in Bristol. London's Conservation Areas are very heavily concentrated in the centre and westwards along the River Thames, including significant parts of some of the suburbs.

The geographic distribution of Conservation Areas reflects both the pattern of London's growth and the policy objectives of designation, namely the protection and enhancement of the character and appearance of areas of particular architectural or historic interest. Within central London, Conservation Areas include the diplomatic quarters of Kensington, concentrations of major public buildings, areas of historic residential development, the Royal Parks, distinctive quarters such as the Inns of Court, and long-established commercial areas such as Clerkenwell and Soho. Outside the centre, Conservation Areas are often designated to protect the centres of old towns and villages which became engulfed by the growing city, such as Highgate Village and Blackheath. Also covered are the open spaces of historic importance, such as the Royal Parks at Greenwich, Richmond, Bushy, parts of Epping Forest and Enfield Chase, and model residential developments including Bedford Park and Hampstead Garden Suburb.

Individual buildings of architectural or historic interest also contribute to the historic built environment. The particular richness of London's historic resource is demonstrated by the relatively high concentration of the nation's Listed Buildings in the capital, ie 35,000 of almost 450,000 in England, or 8%. The majority of these buildings are listed as Grade II, with around 4% at Grade II* and around 2% at Grade I. These proportions reflect the national picture.

Not surprisingly, the highest concentrations of listed buildings are found in central London, with Westminster containing over a quarter of the London total and Kensington and Chelsea, Islington, and Camden each containing over 10% (see Table 1). The only other boroughs containing more than 5% of the London total are Lambeth and Tower Hamlets. However, the contribution of listed buildings to the local historic environment in other areas must not be

Fig 3 Christchurch, Spitalfields

underestimated as their value as rare examples of buildings of architectural or historic interest may be enhanced by the local context.

In addition to buildings listed by the Department of National Heritage (formerly the Department of the Environment), 24 boroughs maintain lists of buildings of local interest and a further three are either considering or are preparing such a list (see Table 2). Currently over 15,000 buildings in London are included on local lists and over 3,000 are provisionally included. With the exception of Richmond, the boroughs with the highest number of locally listed buildings are located in inner London, namely Islington, Greenwich, Hammersmith and Fulham, Hackney, and Wandsworth. However the majority of boroughs without a local list are those in central London which have high numbers of statutorily listed buildings, reflecting a reliance on the formal listing process.

London is rich in places of worship of historic or architectural interest. The majority of these are churches of the Church of England, although there are many examples of places of worship of other denominations and faiths which have considerable historic or architectural value. Churches have, until recently, been graded in much the same way as listed buildings, using three categories of importance. Grades A, B, and C are largely commensurate with the secular Grades I, II*, and II. English Heritage is currently resurveying listed buildings across England and churches are gradually being re-classified according to the secular system. Consequently, comparing London with the national picture at present is not useful.

Fig 4 Lonsdale Square, Islington

Fig 5 St James's Park, Westminster (Photo Greater London Record Office Photographic Collection)

Most of these churches of historic or architectural interest are located in central and inner London, reflecting both the importance of religion during the early growth of the capital and the special contribution of church architecture to local street scenes and townscapes. There are also churches of historic or architectural interest in many outer London boroughs, usually located in old town and village centres. London also has some specific building forms. One of the most important is the 'London Square'. Eight inner London boroughs contain over 200 London Squares, as designated by the London Squares Preservation Act 1931.

Landscape and open space
One of the most striking features of London's historic environment is the number and range of gardens included on the *Register of Historic Parks and Gardens* (EH 1984-6). Out of a total of 1200 entries in England, some 10% are located in London. Many small examples are found in central London while larger examples tend to be located throughout the capital, with a heavier representation in the west than in the east. Their distribution reflects the location of royal hunting grounds, the later search for retreats from city life, and the laying out of open space as part of speculative residential developments. Examples include Bushy Park, the gardens at Hampton Court, Greenwich Park, and Finsbury Park. This component of the historic environment is included on the map in Fig 1.

At a wider scale, areas of Heritage Land, as proposed by the Countryside Commission and the Nature Conservancy Council, have also been included in Fig 1. This definition promotes the protection of extensive areas of open land particularly significant to London by virtue of their landscape, historic, and nature conservation interest. Their location is very strongly biased towards existing areas of undeveloped land to the north and south of the main built-up areas of London, including Epping Forest, Rainham Marshes, Joyden's Wood, and Bushy Park.

Areas of Special Character, as defined in the Greater London Development Plan 1976, are also included in Fig 1. These areas were considered to contribute to the special character of London as a whole and include open tracts of land of high landscape value, outstanding village and town centres, the most important central precincts, most of the length of the Thames within Greater London, and some areas of exceptional architectural and historic interest. Land identified as Areas of Special Character included most of the areas proposed as Heritage Land, with the addition of the Thames and large areas of Richmond and Wimbledon, Dulwich village, and Westminster. In addition, around half of the London boroughs have defined local areas of special character (see

Fig 6 Kings Cross looking south from the Regent's Canal, Camden

Table 2). These cover various aspects of the local environment which are considered to be important by virtue of their special residential or townscape character, or landscape value. Interpretation of the definition varies between boroughs with around half using Conservation Area-type criteria for their definition, while others reflect landscape or residential quality or a combination of the aspects listed above. Kensington and Chelsea, for example, consider the heritage and landscape value of an area as well as the use to which areas are put, whereas Newham and Ealing use Conservation Area-type criteria.

Views

An essential element of London's environment are the views to and from particular places and buildings . Seventeen of the London boroughs recognise strategic views as defined by the Government in PPG 3 (DOE 1989a). Many of the boroughs also identify important local views, either through a general Unitary Development Plan (UDP) policy or by identifying specific views to be protected. In the case of Kensington and Chelsea local views are not referred to in the UDP but in supplementary planning guidance. Generally, policies to protect strategic views apply in inner

London boroughs and the City of London. This is explained by the particular importance of some central London structures, notably St Paul's Cathedral and the Palace of Westminster. However, there does not seem to be any particular pattern to the interpretation of local views.

Table 3 Distribution of scheduled ancient monuments

Borough	number
Barking & Dagenham	1
Barnet	2
Bexley	3
Brent	0
Bromley	8
Camden	1
City	55
Croydon	4
Ealing	6
Enfield	5
Greenwich	9
Hackney	0
Hammersmith & Fulham	1
Haringey	0
Harrow	7
Havering	3
Hillingdon	5
Hounslow	7
Islington	2
Kensington & Chelsea	3
Kingston	7
Lambeth	0
Lewisham	0
Merton	3
Newham	2
Redbridge	0
Richmond	6
Southwark	7
Sutton	6
Tower Hamlets	7
Waltham Forest	1
Wandsworth	1
Westminster	4

Note: Figures correct at March 1992. At July 1994 there were 166 SAMs in Greater London.
Source: English Heritage, 1994

Archaeology

The historic environment of London also includes those areas below ground level which contain remnants of past activity. Areas of Archaeological Priority or Significance cover large areas of London, particularly in the centre and along the Thames and routes of old roads and rivers. Parts of old villages and towns which have not had potential archaeological areas of interest disrupted by deep foundations are also included in these areas. The pattern of these areas reflects the way in which London grew up from the City of London and Westminster, engulfing smaller settlements over time.

In addition some sites and monuments have been identified as being of historic, architectural, artistic, or archaeological interest. These are listed on county Sites and Monuments Records (SMRs). The SMR in London is managed by English Heritage and currently holds around 60,000 entries. One category of items included on the SMR is Scheduled Ancient Monuments (SAMs), monuments considered to be of national importance. English Heritage is currently undertaking a review of SAMs, making a comparison of figures for London with the English total difficult. However, out of the 166 SAMs in Greater London there is a particularly heavy concentration located in the City (see Table 3). This reflects the earliest origins of London, as the majority of Roman, and earlier, finds come from this area.

The evolution of London

London's claim to uniqueness has been particularly powerful since the eighteenth century. Historic descriptions of London abound in expressions of astonishment at the city's character. The commonest themes in these accounts are London's massive size, complexity and diversity, its commercial energy, the special nature of its housing, and the appalling pollution it suffered from coal smoke. Not all of these features are still relevant. Though very large, London is far from being the biggest world metropolis today, and though it suffers still from pollution, the coal smoke and the fogs that went with it are gone. However, complexity, diversity, commercial dynamism, and an internationally-admired tradition of housing are all still recognisable.

Among the various books extolling London, one has special relevance to this report, Steen Eiler Rasmussen's *London: the unique city* (1934), written over sixty years ago but still read and respected. Rasmussen offered the first architect-planner's-eye view of London as a whole. His historical and geographical analysis was of a metropolis which had spread out rapidly from two centres, the City and Westminster. Because development had been piecemeal and at low densities, the individuality of the many villages absorbed by London had been preserved. Building development and control in London, he believed, had reflected the evolving form of British democracy. In his architectural evaluation, Rasmussen admired the squares, the parks, the suburbs, and the housing of London. He was impressed by the standard of London's public transport, which was just becoming co-ordinated , and he saw this service as a means to extending London's low-density housing, which he regarded as 'humane' in comparison with the flatted blocks of other great cities. London's major buildings reached no very elevated standards, he felt, but he found that the average standards of construction, common sense and comfort in London were high, from which other cities could learn.

Conditions have changed in many ways since Rasmussen wrote, but the view he expressed still has special importance. In particular, Rasmussen's conception of London as a decentralised city of linked villages has now become common currency. Such has been his influence that this has come to embody what many people feel about London. London's physical characteristics today could be expressed in this summary of some essential features. London is a great capital city with all the ceremonial and institutional buildings and features which that entails. It is also a great commercial city with a building stock that must be adapted or renewed to meet the changing nature of commerce. It is a city with a powerful and honoured tradition of housing at low density, both in central areas and in the suburbs. Its suburbs, consisting of both the old villages now absorbed in the metropolis and the many new developments between and around them, reach a standard of urban quality unequalled in any world city. London has an enviable reputation for open space and for the quality and variety of its parks, squares, and other landscapes. In the range of its environments it is a more various and less monotonous city than practically any other world metropolis. It is a city famed for its picturesque and unexpected effects and outlines more than for the formal and consistent gestures of planning so often equated with successful urban architecture.

The study shows that these special characteristics of London are still reflected in the fabric and nature of its historic environment. That may help to assess more precisely the contribution that London's historic environment makes to the welfare and success of the metropolis today. The 'historic environment' is, of course, hard to specify. One person's sense of historic or architectural value will differ from another's and such sentiments merge with vaguer cultural or social values like 'community', 'atmosphere', or 'individuality'. The discussion that follows is inevitably partial. The omission of any generic type of building should not be taken to mean that it has a lesser value, as exceptions often have rarity value. The aim here is to focus upon what is typical and has done most for London's reputation as a whole.

The earliest urban centres of London,

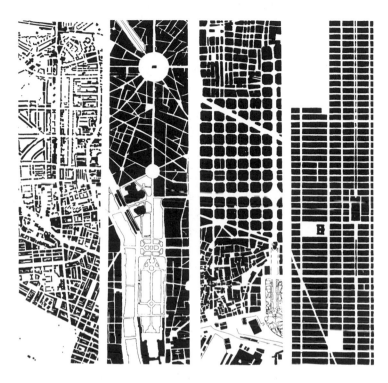

Fig 7 Illustration of four city plans (left to right London, Paris, Barcelona, and Manhattan) from A guide to the architecture of London by Jones and Woodward

namely the City of London, Westminster, and portions of Southwark possess a special value by virtue of their antiquity. The sense of London as a Roman and medieval city is chiefly focused upon these quarters. Little of the Roman period can be seen above ground apart from much-renewed stretches of the City Wall, yet a half-submerged consciousness of London's nearly 2,000 years of history can be argued to be critical to its pride and identity. Ancient monuments and sites of archaeological value are widely scattered throughout London, and are a popular source of local enthusiasm and initiative , but there is a natural concentration of interest in the 'central business district'. The string of discoveries made in recent years, such as the gradual uncovering of the Roman forum and the finding of an amphitheatre under Guildhall Yard, have confirmed that London was no outpost but a significant city of the Roman Empire. This helps, in subtle ways, to boost London's standing as a world city. These central districts also possess the finest of London's medieval buildings. They vary from such sources of national veneration, foreign revenue, and architectural beauty as Westminster Abbey, the Tower of London, and Southwark Cathedral to less-visited churches like St Bartholomew the Great and St Helen's Bishopsgate. Like the Roman discoveries, these medieval survivals play a special role in London's consciousness and self-confidence. Outer boroughs also have former village churches of comparable antiquity, smaller in scale but fundamental in moulding local identity.

Another group of structures with special

Fig 8 St Mary Woolnoth, City of London

Fig 9 St James's Palace, Westminster

value and character are the City churches, notably the surviving so-called 'Wren churches' built after the Great Fire of 1666, together with St Paul's Cathedral. Many suffered grievously in the Second World War, others have an insecure future, and most have been dwarfed in scale by modern developments. Yet collectively they are of great symbolic moment in a part of London where commercial efficiency is regarded as a vital, if not the only, imperative. In some areas they are the only visible reminder of the City's venerable history. With them can be grouped the City's other remaining buildings of outstanding value, the Bank of England, the Royal Exchange and so on. On the fringes of the City, the Inns of Court are London's closest equivalent to the collegiate, quadrangular model of British architecture so much admired and visited at Oxford and Cambridge. They contain buildings of the greatest interest and variety, stretching from the Romanesque Temple Church to post-war neo-Georgian development.

Apart from the specific types of building mentioned above, the City and its environs are rich still in a picturesque environmental quality found often in London and best denominated as 'surprise'. This subtle quality depends on many factors, among them intimacy, obscurity, accident, and a contrast of scales in streets and buildings. It is something that can rarely be achieved by conscious planning, yet it is very vulnerable to insensitive changes to the streetscape. Undoubtedly, the intimacy still to be savoured in the smaller courts and yards of these central quarters of London, in contrast to the big buildings along the main thoroughfares, is valued by its inhabitants as highly as the elegance of particular monuments.

High on the list of London's unique attractions are the royal palaces. The main surviving examples, in rough chronological order, are the Tower of London, Eltham, Greenwich, Hampton Court, St James', the Banqueting House of Whitehall Palace, Kensington Palace, Buckingham Palace, and the Palace of Westminster itself. Their value for London depends partly on their history and symbolism, partly on their number, and partly on their range of character. No other world city enjoys such a diversity of palaces. Their link with a continuing monarchy adds to their appeal both for Londoners and tourists.

Closely allied with the royal palaces are the parks, always an admired feature of central London. London's reputation for generous green space is premised on its central parks. These are mostly royal, St James', Green Park, Hyde Park and Kensington Gardens, and Regent's Park (a special case because it is tied in with the famous Nash development around its

Fig 11 St Saviour's Dock, Shad Thames, Southwark

Fig 10 Highgate Cemetery, Camden

fringes and includes the London Zoo). The variety and freshness of landscape and architecture in these parks are as great an asset to London as their number. Hardly less important parks and large open spaces

a little further from the centre include Battersea Park, Hampstead Heath, Victoria Park, Clissold Park, and Finsbury Park. Then there are large royal parks further out at Greenwich, Richmond, and Bushy , a medley of grounds belonging to former country houses or large villas, picturesque early cemeteries at Highgate, Kensal Green, Brompton, Nunhead, West Norwood, and Stoke Newington, and a multitude of smaller open spaces, some specially laid out by local authorities, others formed from old burial grounds. In each of these, the English genius for informal landscape, gardening, and the occasional modest building or feature finds individual expression. Parks and open spaces come high on the list of amenities valued by visitors to London and by foreign residents.

The Thames is London's time-honoured axis. It has been the historic source of its wealth and its prime means of transport. Most of the royal palaces stand along its banks, as do many other historic houses and outstanding buildings of all

Fig 13 Southgate Underground Station, Enfield

Fig 12 Regent's Canal, Camden

kinds such as Lambeth Palace, Somerset House, Ham House, County Hall, the South Bank Arts Centre, the Tate Gallery, and Battersea and Bankside Power Stations. The Thames bridges contribute much to the sense of an historic river. The oldest today is Richmond Bridge. Two, Tower Bridge and Albert Bridge, are powerfully picturesque structures. Less visibly, the tunnels, notably the Thames Tunnel from Rotherhithe to Shadwell, have their place in the history of engineering. The enclosed docks built between 1800 and 1930 east of the Tower were also objects of great scale, power, and originality, much admired and visited in their day. The demolition of so much of them in the last thirty years has been a grievous loss to London's architectural heritage. Better use and appreciation of the Thames is an old theme in planning policies for London. From the visitors' point of view the Thames cannot be said to be neglected or unloved, since guided river trips are so popular. The margins of the river are always interesting between Battersea Bridge and Tower Bridge. Between Lambeth Bridge and Blackfriars Bridge the North Bank is consistently splendid, with the Houses of Parliament, the outstanding public building of the nineteenth century, dominant, the prospect at its best perhaps from Waterloo Bridge. Above Battersea Bridge and below Tower Bridge the general quality is less high, though there are fine riparian stretches at Greenwich downstream, and at Chiswick, Mortlake, Kew, Richmond, and Ham upstream.

As well as the Thames, London also has valuable secondary rivers such as the Wandle, the Crane, and the Lea, a number of canals including the Regent's Canal and the Grand Union Canal, and the remarkable aqueduct of the New River.

Fig 14 St Pancras Station, Camden

Fig 15 The New Cross Inn, New Cross Road, Lewisham

These are increasingly appreciated environmental assets in themselves and boast fine structures at intermittent points along their length.

London's railway infrastructure is of great historic and architectural importance. Britain was the first country to develop railways, and London is home to some internationally outstanding early railway architecture. The demolition of the Euston Arch in 1961 was a sore loss. However, among the early termini, Paddington with its iron train shed by Brunel survives, as do King's Cross, St Pancras, and the main Liverpool Street train shed. These are the outstanding monuments to early iron architecture in London, rivalled only by the glasshouses in Kew Gardens and a few market buildings like Covent Garden. Contemporary with St Pancras was the beginning of the world's first underground railway. Portions of the original stations remain along the

Fig 16 The Natural History Museum, Cromwell Road, Kensington and Chelsea

Circle Line, but the sections of the underground system most admired are the stations built under the aegis of Charles Holden between 1924 and 1939. These include some very handsome examples in outlying boroughs, particularly on the Piccadilly Line. The coherence and clarity of design for bus and underground which so impressed Rasmussen and others in the 1930s have recently been much eroded and a piecemeal approach has found favour, to the serious detriment of London's unity of image.

Of the West End's public attractions, the most valuable as historic buildings are the theatres, the pubs, and the museums. Theatres are critical to London's cultural reputation, and the Theatres Trust watches vigilantly over their welfare. Most of the West End's working theatres are Victorian or later, though Drury Lane goes back to 1812. Here is a sizeable collection of expressive, lively, and individual buildings still in the original, popular use for which they were built. Most have unexpectedly small though highly ornamented auditoria, which helps to promote a particular style of English acting. Outer areas of London also have a flourishing theatrical life, often in fine listed buildings such as the Hackney Empire and the Richmond Theatre.

Pubs of architectural quality are fairly widely scattered across London. Though valued by Londoners and visitors alike, they are too often taken for granted. Surprisingly few are listed buildings, since many date from the 1890s or later and many have been much altered. The range of pub architecture is broad, from remnants of coaching inns like the George in Southwark through gin palaces like the Salisbury in St Martin's Lane to the Tabard, a cottagey 'reform' pub in

Fig 17 All Saints, Margaret Street, Westminster (Photo Martin Charles)

Bedford Park. Some other British cities boast a richer array of gin palaces, but none has London's diversity. There are, it goes without saying, no true equivalents abroad.

London has a vast resource of museums and galleries, often housed in buildings of outstanding architectural merit. The two most important cultural concentrations are at South Kensington and the South Bank. In both places architectural and cultural initiatives are pending. South Kensington boasts four Victorian buildings of the highest quality, the Victoria and Albert Museum and the Natural History Museum at one end of the complex, the Albert Hall and the Albert Memorial at the other. The South Bank is more linear in character, and its buildings are more recent, but it is beginning now to be revalued after years of unpopularity. Large museums or galleries of international repute for their contents, but also of special value for their architecture or setting, include the National Gallery (linked to the subtler National Portrait Gallery), the British Museum, and the Tate Gallery. Many smaller cultural

Fig 18 Deptford Town Hall, Lewisham

Fig 19 Marylebone Fire Station, Chiltern Street, Westminster

institutions, like the Dulwich Picture Gallery and the Horniman Museum in South London, or the Whitechapel Gallery and Geffrye Museum in the East End, could also be cited. The contribution made by buildings for the arts to the vitality, economy, and amenity of cities is now recognised. Most of London's local museums are housed in listed buildings, often houses or other structures of much historic or architectural interest.

Many other specialised types of building and structure offer something distinctive to London's environment. Churches have always been a prime focus of architectural and artistic endeavour. London's places of worship are too varied to categorise simply. In outlying boroughs, as in the City, there are important medieval churches, and the Wren churches have been mentioned above. Central London boasts three subsequent groups of Anglican churches of special importance. First are the new churches of Queen Anne's reign, of which the half dozen or so by Hawksmoor reach the highest rank of architectural quality. Then come the so-called Commissioners Churches, built between about 1818 and 1835, usually in the Greek style, and often landmarks for inner-city areas. Lastly there are the many Victorian Gothic churches, which are often endowed with beautiful fittings. The towers and steeples of these different churches give a public or civic dimension to their architecture. The Church of England has difficulty in keeping many of its London churches in operation, and radical changes to their sensitive interiors are far commoner than they used to be. Other denominations all have outstanding buildings in London, from Bevis Marks Synagogue on the fringe

Fig 20 Essendine School, Essendine Road, Westminster

of the City to the Methodist Central Hall and the Westminster Cathedral at opposite ends of Victoria Street.

London can claim a range of government and municipal buildings unequalled anywhere except perhaps Paris and New York. Central government buildings of the first rank, like the Foreign and Commonwealth Office or the Admiralty, are secure. London's town halls, mostly the product of the period 1890-1940 and a powerful focus still for local identity and loyalty, are important too. Many fine town halls in places like Deptford and Hampstead which ceased to be local authorities in 1965, are now inadequately used and esteemed, and some have been or are being sold off. The case of County Hall, for eighty years a symbol of London's pride and identity, is the most alarming instance of this trend.

In addition, many types of London building erected during the heyday of local government have special appeal and character but are under growing threat due to changes in the provision of public services. One such instance is the 'board school', whose tall but friendly appearance stands out all over the inner boroughs and often rivals churches as a local landmark. Then there is the branch public library, more often than not housed in a late Victorian or Edwardian building of quality, the Edwardian or inter-war police station or fire station, and the old-style public baths, a type in some danger of extinction. Generally, the buildings erected by the London County Council and the London Boroughs in the earlier years of their existence are of high quality. Many are now listed buildings, but alternative uses have increasingly to be found for them.

With changes in methods of health care a significant number of London hospitals are becoming redundant or facing major changes. Some such as Barts and Guy's have conferred a distinct identity on certain quarters and enjoy long historical associations. Elsewhere, at Friern Barnet,

Fig 22 New End Hospital, Camden

Barnet, Highlands, Enfield, and Claybury in Redbridge, beneficial new uses are needed for huge complexes of fine Victorian buildings which are local landmarks. In each case, effective conservation strategies are required.

As has been noted, the relationship between commerce, industry, and the quality of London's built environment has frequently been difficult. The average standard of its office buildings for instance, is not high, despite notable exceptions, such as the early twentieth-century Imperial classical buildings of Regent Street, Piccadilly, Kingsway/Aldwych, and parts of the City of London.

This sense of a London of specialised quarters can be extended. The greatest and most enduring of all quarters (which shows no signs of diminishing despite periodic fears), is the City of London financial district itself. Others are the retailing strips along Oxford Street from Tottenham Court Road to Marble Arch,

Fig 21 Claybury Hospital, Manor Road, Redbridge

and Regent Street. The diplomatic district of Mayfair, Belgravia, and South Kensington is, in a different sense, another trade quarter that shows little sign of shifting. Here there is greater compatibility with the historic environment. The government quarter of Whitehall includes some of London's finest historic buildings such as the Banqueting House and the Foreign Office, and cultural quarters include South Kensington (museums) and the South Bank (arts and entertainment). In both, historic architecture has a key role to play in activities which are in many ways a form of transaction or trade. In ethnic quarters, like the Bangladeshi district of Brick Lane in Spitalfields or 'Chinatown' around Gerrard Street in the West End, a traditional London street-scene is overlaid and enriched with the trappings of another culture but not fundamentally transformed. The contribution of street

Fig 23 Australia House, Strand, Westminster

markets and antique markets for instance Portobello Road in North Kensington, Chapel Market/Camden Passage in Islington, and Camden Lock in Camden Town, is of the same nature.

In terms of districts, the whole of

Fig 25 Camden Lock Market

London's centre, from South Kensington in the west to the Tower in the east, and from the Euston Road/Marylebone Road/City Road line in the north to the South Bank of the Thames, can be said to possess strategic rather than local interest. Here lies the core of central London today. Outside it, every borough has ancient monuments and historic buildings of outstanding quality, and, as has been said, the general standard of design and amenity of the twentieth-century London suburbs is high. It may nevertheless be helpful to identify certain areas beyond the centre with specially high standards and expectations of environmental quality.

Chief among these are the old village centres of outer London, those large and strong enough to have resisted loss of identity when London encroached upon them. Outstanding in this category are Greenwich to the south-east, Hampstead

Fig 24 Entrance to Chinatown

and Highgate to the north, and Richmond to the south-west. All four of these 'inner-outer' suburbs have long been connected with London, but enjoyed some special status so that they flourished as handsome, prosperous communities and retained open land around them. The character of their centres is in every case picturesque and distinctive. Other centres at about the same radius from London are less attractive but almost as important. An example is Woolwich, battered by war and redeveloped but long associated with the Army and endowed with some striking military buildings. There are also smaller centres of outstanding quality like Blackheath, Dulwich, or Kew Green. What marks out these outlying centres is a mixture of fine buildings at all sorts of scales, informal layout, and ample open space with plenty of mature trees.

Beyond these and other 'inner-outer' centres lies an outer tier of communities, often well-developed as towns before they become part of London. Many are still not wholly reconciled to their metropolitan identity. Such, for instance, are Barking, Bromley, Croydon, Enfield, Kingston, and Romford. They vary greatly in attractiveness, and in the attitude that the respective borough authorities have taken to conservation. Nearly all have isolated buildings of exceptional quality, and in most of these outer boroughs one finds major houses, monuments, or historic areas of one kind or another which have been caught up in London's outward expansion. A happy feature of the outer boroughs are villages where a village character is proudly preserved still. Such for instance are Harmondsworth in Hillingdon, Harrow-on-the-Hill (where the linear nature of the famous public school helps to create an outstanding ensemble), Hayes in Bromley, and Carshalton in Sutton.

Less remarked upon is the good-quality planning and architecture of some of the inter-war brick-built shopping centres in

Fig 26 Mill Hill Village, Barnet

the outer suburbs, especially in North London, as at Southgate, Hendon, and Golders Green. Often linked to a tube station, they manifest the 'good manners' of British suburban architecture of these decades, but enjoy a better sense of scale and coherence than many of the housing developments that they serve. Few of them

Fig 27 Fortis Green Road, Haringey

Fig 28 Queen Anne's Gate, Westminster

have yet been considered for Conservation Area designation, since Conservation Areas in London's outer boroughs are not often designated outside residential areas.

It was mentioned above that London is noted above all for the special and successful character of its housing. The building type most indigenous and original to London is the narrow-fronted, brick-built town house, intended for a single family. The proliferation of this type in different variants has given London a great sense of individuality. It has remained generally popular for three and a half centuries.

The London town house has gone through a long evolution. Narrow-fronted timber houses were the norm in London streets before the Reformation. In the seventeenth century brick was substituted for timber, and after the Great Fire construction became standardised to cope with the emerging building regulations. At first, brick houses of this type tended to be built in twos or threes at most, not in real 'terraces', a term originating in the mid-Georgian period. They came at every scale and performed every function. In other words, they were not just houses, but offices, pubs, shops, and workshops as well. They were built along streets, in small yards and alleys, and as ribbon development along main roads. Behind the house was nearly always a modicum of private space, critical to the London house tradition. At the least it might be used as a back yard for washing or trade, at its best it could be a ample garden. Few London town houses dating from before 1700 now remain. They become commoner thereafter (Queen Anne's Gate in Westminster has some superb early examples) and survive in ever larger numbers after 1720. As building becomes better capitalised, more are built at a time. Gradually they begin to be grouped in 'terraces' and, after 1770, grand urban compositions.

Linked with the growth of the London town house is the tradition of the London Square, with facades grouped round an open space. It begins as a feature of the seventeenth-century West End suburbs. The Piazza of Covent Garden is the first celebrated example, though now successfully adapted to later uses. As a space, Lincoln's Inn Fields is better preserved. The early West End squares (Bloomsbury, Red Lion, St James's, Soho) retain their physical form and amenity but little of their original buildings or landscape. In combination with the terrace, the London Square (and later variants such as the crescents) proved both popular and elastic. It became the backbone of fashionable estate development, and can be found in all the inner suburbs, most copiously perhaps in Kensington, Bloomsbury, and Islington. It is a measure of its significance that legislation to protect London squares was brought in as early as 1931 with the London Squares Preservation Act. The variety of London squares is infinite. Bedford Square and Fitzroy Square are the best preserved of the mid-Georgian squares, and, among later examples, the chains of squares in Islington, notably Milner Square, Cloudesley Square, and Lonsdale Square, stand out.

The next phase in the development of the London town house was to set it in a picturesque landscape and break up terraces into blocks or components of varying scale, comprising terraces, semi-detached houses, and villas, sometimes with an informal road layout. As perfected

Fig 29 Gibson Square, Islington

by Nash at Regent's Park, this became London's nineteenth-century answer to suburban dwelling. The villa form was soon taken up in developments for the

Fig 31 Lloyd Square, Islington

Fig 30 Claremont Square, Islington

Fig 32 Hampstead Garden Suburb, Barnet

wealthy, at St Johns Wood and Maida Vale, for instance, but perhaps Kensington Palace Gardens of the 1840s and '50s is the outstanding example. At the same time, the landscaping of squares and public spaces became denser and more naturalistic. In some parts of London, notably North Kensington, an ingenious arrangement of common gardens behind villas and terraces became popular after

1850. Building styles in this period grow richer and more romantic, and in some developments abandon the classical idiom of the terrace house tradition entirely.

The last clear phase of invention in London housing is the evolution of the garden suburb type of house. This began as a movement to improve the amenities of the smaller suburban house and make it look more picturesque. Bedford Park of the 1870s sees the start of the process. It is taken up with renewed attention by Parker and Unwin at Hampstead Garden Suburb. Here, fresh ideas about road layout and grouping houses in short runs, with more space in front and behind, are combined with revised plans for the two-storey house or cottage. The 'cottagey' nature of these small houses makes it look as though they have little in common with the old tall London house, but essentially they are an adaptation of that tradition to the lower density layouts possible in outer London. It is from Hampstead Garden Suburb and similar developments, eg Brentham in Ealing, that the semi-detached houses ubiquitous in the inter-war suburbs derive.

The London domestic tradition is not confined to the individual house. Flats, once they started to be built in London after 1850, have always been popular, whether they were working-class tenements or middle-class mansion blocks. Flats for the middle classes tended to be confined to the richer districts. Imposing examples in a Queen Anne revival or French style all over Kensington, the West End, St Johns Wood, and Maida Vale help vary the scale of these districts, but are rarely so dominant as to make the streetscape dreary, as in the long boulevards of many European cities. After 1920 they go 'modern' in style, reaching architectural maturity in Lubetkin's two Highpoint blocks at the summit of

Fig 33 Flats on the Millbank Estate, Westminster (Photo Greater London Record Office Photograph Collection)

Highgate. Tenements for the poor are at first raw, flat-roofed brick buildings built round asphalted courts by Victorian philanthropic trusts. They were externally transformed by the London County Council's architects in the 1890s, notably on the Boundary Street and Millbank estates. 'Council flats' lapse back into banality in the inter-war period, only to enjoy a revival in numbers and alternative methods of design in the great public housing boom of the 1950s and '60s.

The best housing of the post-war period shows the London domestic tradition as fertile as ever. Initiatives such as the Span estates at Ham and Blackheath and the mixed development public housing estates at Rochampton and Churchill Gardens, Pimlico, or, a decade later, the high-density concrete megastructures of Alexandra Road, Kilburn, and the Brunswick Centre, Bloomsbury, testify to the special place that housing holds in English architectural thought. Taken as a continuum over the past 300 years, the standard of these achievements in housing cannot be matched in other great cities. They are probably London's greatest single contribution to architecture and planning.

Conclusions

By combining a review of planning designations and definitions with a description of the evolution of the capital London's historic environment can be defined. What emerges is a picture of a rich historic environment of which we should be proud and keen to safeguard. However the attempt at a definition of this sort has highlighted three important issues which should be addressed. The first is the degree to which the criteria for making conservation designations and definitions are interpreted and applied consistently on a London-wide basis. For example, large swathes of London's suburbs fail to achieve any form of

Fig 34 Alexandra Road Estate, Camden

recognition, as does much of the open land on the eastern and western edges of the metropolis.

The second issue relates to the totality of London's historic environment being more than the sum of its parts. There is an inherent danger in only considering the historic environment as being those parts of Greater London which have achieved some form of recognition that is, a designation or definition. The description of the evolution of London illustrates a richness and diversity, the cumulative value of which is not always apparent from designations and definitions.

The description of the evolution of London also highlights the third issue. A recurring theme is the gradual, incremental erosion of the quality and character of some parts of London's historic environment. The conclusion is that while existing systems of control have played a significant role in curbing the worst excesses, some damaging changes are still occurring, particularly as a result of insensitive traffic and highway works and the inability to control the cumulative impact of minor changes to buildings in Conservation Areas.

3 The value of conservation in London

One of the main assumptions about conservation in London is that it protects and creates value. This report investigates this assumption by considering the concept of value from three perspectives, environmental, social, and economic. In each case the nature of the value established is based on the evidence available, including some detailed case study work.

Environmental value

London's historic environment is an invaluable record of our past. Parliament has legislated for its protection because it represents some of the highest achievements of our culture and is a source of national pride. Alternatively, to the majority of Londoners, the value of conservation lies in the contribution it

Fig 36 Butler's Wharf and the Anchor Brewhouse, Shad Thames, Southwark

makes to the quality of the urban environment, creating a diverse urban fabric and differentiating the character of one area from another.

Quality in the urban fabric can be attributed to a number of factors, such as design excellence, form, layout, construction, eyecatching landmarks, or reference points identified with famous people or events, enriching large open spaces and the River Thames, or simply the

Fig 35 Ballast Quay, Greenwich

Fig 37 Butler's Wharf, Shad Thames, Southwark

presence of so many rare and authentic features of great age. However, the value of individual elements and their interactions is important, the total being more than the sum of the parts.

Materials used are also important. Almost by definition, they must be of quality, because they have endured the test of time. Variety is historically as well as geographically interesting. London Bridge and the steps of St Paul's, for example, are constructed from granite taken from vast quarries in Dartmoor and Guernsey respectively.

The contribution of the historic environment to the overall quality of London's urban environment is clearly borne out in the recent LPAC report *London's urban environmental quality* (1993a). This found that environmental quality was affected positively by the application of firm conservation policies, and negatively by the erosion of the historic urban grain. In general terms, the study concluded that 'history and heritage are often the most obvious criteria for defining areas with a clear identity and inherent high urban quality'.

The environmental value of conserving London's historic environment, however, extends far beyond aesthetics, or any of the other attributes mentioned above. It is also about the wise use of resources and maximising the return on past investments. Put very simply, this means that the continued use or reuse of old buildings is generally more efficient and less wasteful in environmental resource terms, than the development of new buildings.

Traditional methods of costing projects or assets do not often, if at all, take into account the environmental costs and benefits of development either at construction stage or during the life of a building. An alternative method, known as 'whole life accounting' does take these factors into consideration and demonstrates the efficiency of conservation. A typical building, for example, is constructed, stands for around 100 years, and is then demolished. Environmental resources, such as bricks, mortar, and other materials are used in construction. A considerable amount of energy is also used in the extraction and processing of raw materials, in transportation, and in the use of construction machinery and manpower. It has been estimated that between 5% and 10% of the annual UK energy consumption total is in the production of building materials (Connaughton, 1990). There is, therefore, a considerable amount of 'embodied' energy and resources in the historic built environment. Modern buildings, on the whole, have higher levels of embodied energy than historic buildings, because building materials tend to come from further afield and construction processes are more energy-intensive, but modern buildings have shorter useful lives. It is clear that the longer life a building has, the greater the efficiency in the use of embodied energy and natural resources.

In the context of the current debate about sustainable development, this in itself is a very strong argument for conservation. Conserving the historic environment incorporates many of the fundamental principles of sustainability:

- it prevents the irreversible loss of the nation's heritage and maintains and protects important monuments, buildings, sites, and landscape for future generations

- it protects environmental resources that people value

- it promotes prudent use of natural capital ie renewable and non-renewable resources, focusing on reuse and recycling rather than redevelopment

- it encourages a better understanding of our environment through the collection and dissemination of information about our past

Social value

Isolating the 'social' value of conserving London's historic environment, as distinct from its environmental or economic value, is a complex task. It would need separate research which would need to define what is meant by 'social'. For the purposes of this report, 'social' can be defined as being being broadly that which impacts on people and their quality of life.

Buildings, towns, monuments, and other historic features are a fascinating and important educational resource. They are eloquently described in the Environment White Paper *This common inheritance* (DOE 1990): 'They remind us of our past, of how our forebears lived, and how our culture and society have developed. They tell us what earlier generations aspired to and achieved. They provide the context for new buildings, and for changes in our way of life. They teach us lessons for the future.' The Department of the Environment's recent survey of people's views of London produced some interesting findings about the historic environment. The report, *Ten thousand views of London* (DOE 1994d), concluded that people 'are clearly proud of London's rich history and tradition and feel that it contributes significantly to the capital's unique sense of place'. Indeed, 70% of respondents, Londoners and visitors alike, referred to historic buildings, old churches, ceremonies, and pageantry as the features they like most about London.

Nationally, this is reflected in increasing concern for our heritage. There are now over 1000 local amenity societies supported by the Civic Trust and membership of the National Trust has grown from 0.9 to 1.9 million over the last ten years. English Heritage, set up in 1984, had gained 350,000 members ten years later.

The sense of place and identity that historic buildings bring to different areas of London is clearly important. The County of London Plan (1943) identified the old-established towns or villages absorbed by the spread of London, aiming to reinforce their identity. Where the old villages have retained a distinct identity, strong conservation policies have played a part. However, some towns and villages within London have changed over the years, often damaging the historic built environment, with a consequent erosion in their character and identity.

There are very strong arguments now in favour of reviving London's town and village centres as focal points for economic and social life. Government policy, expressed in Planning Policy Guidance note 6 (PPG 6) *Town centres and major retail development* (1993), emphasises the importance of reviving the 'vitality and viability' of town centres, and a recent report published by the DOE describes how this challenge should be met (Department of the Environment 1994a). The DOE report states that traditional, established town centres transmit our culture in a better way than new out-of-town centres ever can, and the research shows that historic town centres have proved to be the most successful for investment. This in turn suggests that historic centres are better able to weather recessions because of their diversity and interest. In addition, research undertaken by Middlesex University for LPAC on *Place and local identity* (unpublished) showed that people relate more strongly to established historic areas than to newer centres or administrative areas. One reason for this is that community buildings, or those that perform a social function, are often historic landmarks in the urban environment. Schools, libraries, churches, and municipal buildings are obvious examples.

The important sense of place and identity created by historic landmark buildings can be seen by looking at parts of London which have developed unconnected with traditional centres. They include areas which have undergone comprehensive redevelopment, often as a result of slum clearance, and large-scale new development on greenfield sites. The social character of these areas is related to a number of factors, one of which is their relative isolation from historic centres and the services they offer for instance the kind of transport, shops, community facilities, and employment available. A further factor, in many cases, is the unbalanced demographic and socio-economic profile of new areas. For example, they may be dominated by one particular age group and as a consequence not have the benefits of a diverse resident population. In contrast, many older historic areas tend to offer a greater range of housing and employment opportunities which in turn can create a better social mix. Typical examples of older buildings offering employment potential in London include redundant industrial buildings converted to craft workshops or studios, and railway arches used for car repairs.

With housing, there is evidence that positive conservation measures, such as the 'living over the shop' initiative, can increase the social mix by attracting younger people to live in central areas previously dominated by pensioners. Jane Jacobs, in *The death and life of great American cities* (1961), makes these points very well. 'Cities need old buildings so badly it is probably impossible for vigorous streets and districts to grow without them. By old buildings, I mean not museum-piece old buildings, not old in an excellent and expensive state of rehabilitation, ... but also a good lot of plain, ordinary, low value buildings, including some run down old buildings.'

Economic value

The economic value of conserving London's historic environment is related to, and in some instances, generated by, the environmental and social factors referred to above. The report assesses the economic value of conservation in London by examining the relationship between conservation and tourism, the performance of listed buildings in the investment property market, the effect of listed building and Conservation Area status on residential property values, and the role of the historic environment in the process of urban regeneration.

Conservation and tourism
London is now one of the most important tourist destinations in the world. According to the London Tourist Board, it attracted seventeen million visits in 1992, of which ten million came from overseas. The term 'visits' refers to visits within the UK by residents and visits to the UK from overseas. The total number of visits to and within the UK as a whole was 114.1 million, with London accounting for some 15% of the total and 54% of the overseas visits. Expenditure by visitors to London in that year was almost £5 billion (ie 27% of the total UK visitor expenditure). There is little doubt that this is an important contribution to the economy of London and of the nation. This figure has increased consistently over the previous ten years.

Fig 38 Tourists at Covent Garden Piazza, Westminster

Fig 39 Offices in Africa House, Kingsway, Camden

Successive overseas visitor surveys, carried out by the British Tourist Authority and the London Tourist Board, confirm that people are attracted to London by its sense of history and heritage (69% in 1993). The 1990 survey indicated that 42% of visits made to London were for 'historic activities', visiting heritage sites, castles, churches, monuments, and so on. This is reflected by the appearance of some historic buildings and monuments on the list of London's attractions which receive over half a million visitors per year, for instance The Tower of London, St Paul's Cathedral, and Westminster Abbey.

Listed buildings in the investment property market

There are only two studies on the economic consequences of listing buildings, both of which were jointly commissioned by English Heritage and the RICS, *The investment performance of listed buildings* (English Heritage and Royal Institution of Chartered Surveyors, 1993), and *The listing of buildings: the effect on value* (Department of National Heritage, English Heritage, and Royal Institution of Chartered Surveyors, 1994). In addition to these, the views of Drivers Jonas' 'Valuation Panel' have also been examined. This panel meets to validate valuations carried out by the firm in accordance with the Royal Institution of Chartered Surveyors' guidelines.

Taking a sample of 300 listed office buildings, of which 160 were in London, *The investment performance of listed buildings* looked at a number of performance indicators; total returns, capital growth, and rental growth. Nationally, pre-1945 buildings performed at least comparably with their modern counterparts and during the recession listed buildings showed greater resilience. Within central London, the differentials in investment performance were smallest, with listed buildings slightly out-performing other groups. Again within central London, historic buildings which have been substantially reconstructed behind their original facades have been in greater demand for rental use than buildings which have not been reconstructed.

Drivers Jonas' Valuation Panel generally concurred with the findings of this study. However, they commented that the results are based on an important but narrow section of the investment property market. Putting the research into a wider context, they explained that the value of listed buildings is generally higher because they are usually smaller, and are more in demand. Listed buildings have high capital values compared with their rent, possibly because of the perception of owners that good listed buildings will always have a relatively strong market following. In general, the institutions and corporations are attracted to listed buildings because of their cachet. Smaller, classic buildings (up to 7,500 square feet) are in demand for company headquarters, as a prestigious setting for the chairman or board of directors. An example is Ford UK's nineteenth-century building in Mayfair, which accommodates only three permanent employees but is used for corporate hospitality. Listed buildings in all areas are popular with professional firms and provide a relatively stable income to the building's owners.

In contrast, *The listing of buildings: the effect on value* examined the extent of the potential effect of listing on the capital value and use of listed buildings and, to a lesser extent, surrounding buildings. The research assessed 'worst case scenarios, where private costs could be expected to be highest, in order to give an estimate of the maximum cost which might be incurred'. The authors make it clear that the cost to owners of listed buildings only represents one aspect of the economics of listing. Set against private costs are the positive benefits of listing, subjects which are considered in detail elsewhere in this report. However, the rationale for this research was that, while the benefits accrue mainly to society and, in some cases, to those who own neighbouring property, the costs of listing fall mainly on the owners of listed buildings.

The researchers looked at listing in Westminster, Bristol, and Manchester. Westminster is significantly different to Bristol and Manchester because it has a relatively high proportion of listed buildings, strong and extensive conservation policies, and the local economy is very buoyant. Interviews were held with various specialist agents, owners, occupiers, and investors. The eleven case studies were considered to be worst-case scenarios in that they involved listed buildings whose owners were intent on partial or total demolition.

The main findings of the study were that conservation laws and policies normally restrict an owner's options in using a site, thereby reducing value. In some circumstances listing of non-residential buildings does reduce their market value and the effect appeared most marked for small buildings located in areas with high development pressure and outside Conservation Areas. Owners of listed buildings know they are extremely unlikely to receive permission to demolish their buildings, and they do not generally know what alterations are restricted by listing. Listing can also be associated with delay in decision-making.

The listing of buildings: the effect on value raises two points relevant to this study. The first is to do with striking the right balance between private costs and wider social, environmental, and economic values. Listing a building is undertaken on behalf of society because that building is deemed to be of historic, architectural, or cultural importance. Conserving such features is of value to society and it therefore seems fair to conclude that any private cost incurred is a price worth paying. This is particularly so given that a private cost to an individual will normally, at some point, be distributed across the economy as a whole.

The second point is that listing might, in certain circumstances, impede the development process, the implication being that the absence of listing might permit a freer development process. This, we feel, should not be interpreted as a justification for not listing. Instead, it highlights the importance of a coherent and consistent approach to listing where all interested parties are made aware of the reasons for listing and the implications of doing so. It also reinforces the importance of maintaining up-to-date and accurate lists to minimise uncertainty.

Fig 42 Residential property market case study areas

selected (see Fig 42), a small area of SW10 to the north of the Fulham Road, in inner London, and part of Wimbledon, in outer London. The research was based on a series of nine structured telephone interviews with estate agents operating in the case study areas. These established the extent to which value or other indicators point to a general appreciation of listed buildings and property in Conservation Areas. Responses to the interviews indicated that, overall, residential property values are significantly enhanced by listed building and Conservation Area status. This was the case in Wimbledon,

Residential property market

The effect of listed building and Conservation Area status on the residential property market was assessed by looking at case study areas within London. The areas were selected because they consisted of similar residential properties, some lying within Conservation Areas and others in areas without such a designation. Apart from conservation policy, other influences on property values in the case study areas were more or less equal.

Following some pilot surveys to identify areas that met these criteria, two areas were

Fig 40 A London street with damaging alterations

Fig 41 A period house with original features and settings retained

where such properties attract a 5-10% premium. Agents believed that this is due to the buyers having greater confidence that the properties will maintain their value, and that the locality will be likely to remain attractive. Other factors include the cachet that the ownership of historic property brings, and the quality of internal features. It was also reported that the effect of Conservation Areas on residential property values is likely to be even higher if there were greater awareness or understanding of the designations. As one estate agent put it '.... its the location and architecture people want'.

The role of conservation in urban regeneration

It is a widely-held view that historic buildings and the process of conservation contribute positively to urban regeneration. This is based on the assumption that residents, shoppers, and business people, as well as tourists, prefer to spend or invest their money in an attractive historic environment. In a highly mobile and relatively affluent society, the quality of the environment is an increasingly significant factor in determining investment patterns.

The need to regenerate the economies of older urban areas is well-established and reflected in planning policy. In recent years the spotlight has turned on town centres, and the need to increase their economic vitality and viability. *Vital and viable town centres: meeting the challenge* (DoE 1994a) gives considerable support for the view that conserving the historic environment is a critical element in town centre regeneration. The reasons for this are that it is pleasant to live and work among historic buildings , they help to create an identity and sense of place, and they offer diverse uses and rental values to the property market.

The DOE report examined some of these points in a case study area. Deptford High Street (see Fig 43) in south east London, was selected because it is currently being regenerated. It is an inner London town centre, with many buildings of historic interest; for many years it had shown signs of social, economic, and physical decline, and it is designated as a Conservation Area.

Deptford is an untypical example because it has been funded by City Challenge (£7.5 million over a five year period from 1992). However, the success of Lewisham's bid for City Challenge reflected a recognition of the value of the area's historic character. Prior to City Challenge, the Borough had commissioned the Civic Trust Regeneration Unit to suggest ways in which the historic built

Fig 43 Deptford High Street, Lewisham

environment in and around the High Street could be part of a regeneration strategy. As part of the case study, we interviewed the manager of the Deptford High Street City Challenge Team, the Chair of the High Street Association, and representatives of the Civic Trust.

The main findings of the role of conservation in the regeneration process were:

• the designation of a Conservation Area (in the early 1970s) focused attention on the problems and opportunities of the area

Fig 44 Location of Deptford High Street

- Conservation Area designation also imposed a duty upon the Borough to look after the area

- pedestrianisation of the High Street in the late 1980s helped to make it a more attractive environment for shopping

- the conversion of upper floors on the High Street to residential units has attracted people to live in the street, which in turn has supported local businesses (reflected in a reduction of shop vacancy rates from 35 in 1990 to 25 in 1994)

- new types of business accommodation have been created within converted industrial buildings at affordable rent levels, stimulating the growth of new 'seed-bed' business activity

- an environment is being created to attract multiple retailers back to the street and existing retailers have been encouraged to invest in their businesses

- new uses have been attracted to the area as a result of the better atmosphere, for example a new art gallery/cafe

- more visitors have been attracted to the area, usually combining a visit to Deptford (for example, to visit St Paul's Church), with a trip to Greenwich

- grant regimes have been established, known as 'block enveloping schemes', where connecting properties have been refurbished and property owners have contributed 15% of the overall costs

- employment has been created: it is estimated, using standard conversion rates, that the first two block enveloping schemes generated approximately 600 construction worker weeks

It is apparent from our study of Deptford High Street that conservation has played, and is still playing, an important role in urban regeneration. The findings demonstrate that, with careful planning and management, vitality and viability can be restored to a town centre that for many years has been in decline. However this is not the end of the story. Deptford City Challenge, along with the London Boroughs of Lewisham and Greenwich and the Greenwich Waterfront Development Partnership, are promoting the Creekside Renewal initiative, aiming to use the unique character and strong identity inherited from Deptford's maritime past as a stimulus for wider area-based regeneration of the Lewisham/Greenwich waterfront.

Conclusions

It is already established that London's historic environment is of value to society and worthy of conservation. Parliament has legislated for its protection because it embodies some of the highest achievements of our culture and is a source of national pride. However, what this chapter illustrates is that the value of conservation goes beyond the aesthetic and spiritual importance of protecting historic buildings, monuments, and spaces, critical though these are. Conservation provides one of the biggest opportunities to give practical expression to sustainability principles and is a key contributor to the economic well-being of London and the nation. Conserving the historic environment also helps to retain a sense of place and identity and maintain balanced, harmonious communities and a diverse mix of uses. Expenditure on the historic built environment needs to be regarded as a long-term investment in the future economic and social well-being of London.

4 Land-use trends and the historic environment

London's urban fabric is not static. It is in a continuous state of change as the city evolves. Many factors have helped to shape what we see today. This chapter reviews some of the main environmental changes in London in recent years, and assesses the effects these have had.

A review of the recent past, however, only tells part of the story. An understanding of how the factors which shaped change will find expression in the future up to the year 2010 should help to define current conservation priorities.

Identifying land-use trends and their effects

Information on land-use trends in the capital was collected from, amongst others, British Rail, London Underground Ltd, the London Boroughs, the Census, LPAC, the Central Statistical Office, the London Research Centre, the Departments of Employment, Environment, and Transport, the London Tourist Board, RICS, English Historic Towns Forum, SERPLAN, HMSO, and the Sports Council. We used this information to identify and assess the impact of changing patterns of land use on London's historic environment. Table 4 (pp 81-3) gives a summary of the analysis under headings of main changes, key land-use implications, and the effect on the historic environment.

Population
In 1939 the population of Greater London was 8.6 million. It fell steadily to 6.7 million in 1981 and then increased slightly during the 1980s to almost 6.8 million in 1991. The movement of people away from inner London after the war was encouraged by Abercrombie's Greater London Plan of 1944, which planned the decentralisation of part of the population to new and expanded towns beyond the Metropolitan Green Belt. The 1980s increase occurred because the rate of inward migration overtook outward migration, a factor largely explained by the employment opportunities created during the relatively buoyant economic conditions in the mid 80s. However, it may be also a reflection of the reversal of the decentralisation policies prevalent in the 1940s, 50s, and 60s. In the mid 1970s there was a perception that the loss of population was weakening London's economy through, for example, out-migration of skilled workers and the relocation of company headquarters. This led to a number of government policy shifts, including the abolition of the Location of Offices Bureau (LOB) and the withdrawal of the New and Expanded Towns Programme.

The movement of people away from central London has placed considerable pressure on towns and villages beyond the Green Belt, generating changes in their fabric and character. Reading is one such example. The reasons cited by people for moving away from London are a mixture of 'push' and 'pull'. The 'push' is the general decline of the environment and services in London, notably in health and education, and the 'pull' is the lure of a cleaner, safer, and more attractive lifestyle elsewhere (for example, see Naughton 1994). Not only do these trends create increased pressure for development in surrounding towns, villages, and countryside, but they also accentuate the physical, social, and economic decline of parts of inner London by moving investment, employment, and economic activity out of the capital.

Transport

The impact of transport

The shape and size of London have evolved as a response to its transport system. Until the construction of the railways London was a compact city. This all changed with the completion of the radial railway network which allowed people to live further from the centre and to commute longer and longer distances to work. By 1930 London had become the centre of a large metropolitan region which was able to function efficiently because of the accessibility of the rail network.

The growth of motorised traffic only began to be a concern during the 1920s and 30s when it was realised that London's road system was ill-equipped to cope with increasing volumes of traffic. Abercrombie recognised this problem and the Greater London Plan (1944) included proposals for a set of high-capacity ring and radial roads to carry longer-distance traffic. Similar proposals re-emerged in the late 60s in the guise of the 'motorway box' proposed by the Greater London Council (GLC). Sandwiched between these proposals was Buchanan's report *Traffic in towns* which was published in 1963. In response to growing car ownership, Buchanan advocated a new urban form comprising a three-tier road hierarchy, and 'environmental areas' from which through traffic would be excluded.

Many road schemes have been completed since Buchanan's plan. Radial motorways bring traffic into Central London and in 1986 the London orbital motorway, the M25, was completed. Investment in transport has not, however, been restricted to roads. The last 20 years have seen, amongst others, the construction of Terminal 4 at Heathrow, the Jubilee Line, the Docklands Light Railway and, most recently, the new international station at Waterloo. However the over-riding impression of London today is of a city choked by the car, whether parked along suburban streets or sitting nose-to-tail on one of the radial motorways. Data on average traffic speeds on main roads in London supplied by the Department of Transport confirms the perception of increasing levels of congestion. They reveal a steady reduction in average traffic speeds. For example, average speeds for the whole of Greater London fell over the period 1968-70 to 1986-90 from 18.6 mph to 16.0 mph, 21.3 mph to 18.9 mph, and 18.6 mph to 16.5 mph during the morning peak, daytime off-peak, and evening peak hours respectively.

Fig 45 Aerial view of King's Cross/St Pancras area (Photo: Ordnance Survey)

The increased levels of traffic and congestion in London are having a severe impact on buildings, on streets, and on the quality of life. Many historic areas have become choked with traffic as more and more vehicles use the roads, creating increased noise, vibration, and pollution. Many new road schemes have required the demolition of historic buildings and, perhaps more significantly, disrupted the unity of historic areas. Red Routes too have generated considerable controversy. Designating a road as a Red Route was intended to reinforce its role as a through route, with measures to control parking and stopping. While average traffic speeds appear to have increased on the Red Routes, local residents and traders are concerned about some of the spin-off effects, including increased noise and pollution, greater safety risks, loss of trade, and displacement of traffic onto side roads. Research sponsored by the Traffic Director for London on the impact of Red Routes on traffic and land use is continuing.

Fig 46 Cabmen's shelter, Kensington Road (Photo: Derek Rowe (Photos) Ltd)

At a more detailed level, the apparent lack of cooperation and integrated action by planners and traffic engineers has led to traffic management schemes which have eroded, rather than enhanced, the quality of the areas they were intended to improve. The physical impact on historic streets and buildings of the hardware of traffic management, signs, road markings, bollards and so on, is often negative, whereas the policy of reducing the volume of traffic should have been a step towards an environmental improvement. These points echo concerns highlighted by the English Historic Towns Forum in *Traffic in historic town centres* (1994). Further, the strong sense of civic order which once characterised many of London's streets has been eroded substantially in recent years by the cumulative impact of streetscape changes, for example the replacement of traditional patterns of staggered rectangular stone or concrete slab paving by ill-considered brick or square block paviours.

Fig 47 Clutter of street furniture

Future transport policy for London

A key to London's future is investment in its transport infrastructure. Both national planning policy guidance on transport (DoE 1994e) and LPAC's *Advice on strategic planning guidance for London* (1994a) point to the overriding need to redress the balance between the private car and other modes of transport if London is to have a sustainable future. Some of the transport infrastructure projects programmed for completion in the next 15 years appear to reinforce this policy objective, whereas with others the likely effects are less clear-cut. The major infrastructure projects are listed in Appendix 2.

LPAC's *Advice* states that investment in public transport, notably rail, will make an important contribution to London's economic growth and well-being by increasing Londoners' accessibility to jobs, services, and activities, as well as maintaining the level of access from the rest of the south-east region. It could be argued that road investment would serve a similar purpose, although PPG 13 reiterates the Government's intention not to build new trunk or local roads simply to facilitate commuting by car into congested urban centres. Assuming the Government's policy intentions will be carried through in practice, transport investment should be targeted at public transport and complementary measures such as better conditions for pedestrians and cyclists, traffic management, reducing car parks, appropriate traffic calming, and so on, and park-and-ride schemes.

A transport strategy to improve accessibility through public transport investment would affect the historic environment in a number of ways, either directly or indirectly, and at national, regional, and local level. Table 5 summarises what this might mean.

Generally, the indirect impacts would be positive, but may create problems if not managed properly. For example, economic growth could create the funds to renovate redundant buildings and bring disused areas back into use. An increase in visitor numbers would also generate funds to invest in historic visitor attractions, with land-use planning accommodating new development appropriately. Locally, increased construction work and more people using the rail network would probably be seen as a necessary but negative effect. The most significant aspect of investment in transport is probably the potential it creates for regeneration. Increasing the accessibility of an area enhances its advantages as a location for business and improves its chances of investment.

Table 5 Effects of public transport investment: impact on the historic environment

level	*direct*	*indirect*
national	–	improved accessibility may facilitate economic growth and lead to an increase in visitor numbers
regional	–	opportunities to harness transport investment to fund regeneration
local	impact on historic streets of complementary street measures, eg signage, materials, furniture, etc	reduced traffic on roads, thereby lessening the impact of cars on historic areas
	loss of historic structures caused by infrastructure development	
	impact on the historic environment of increased use of the rail network	

The list of major infrastructure proposals (Appendix 2) identifies Terminal 5 at Heathrow as a project which may go ahead before 2010 depending on the outcome of the forthcoming public inquiry. It is acknowledged that the investment bias towards the west of London has been a contributory factor to the decline of parts of inner London and much of the area to the east of the region, as noted by LPAC '.... no other single location has such a pervasive influence over London and the South East' (LPAC 1994a). Further development at Heathrow would probably exacerbate the east-west imbalance, possibly leading to overdevelopment in the west and further decline in the east. This may well occur despite the best endeavours to promote the East Thames Corridor as the development opportunity for the future and the various efforts to secure economic regeneration for instance Objective 2 status for the Lea Valley. At the same time, Heathrow is one of London's, and the nation's, international resources, and its ability to cater efficiently for air travellers produces area-wide economic benefits.

In addition to the issues associated with infrastructure, the schemes listed in Appendix 2 are also likely to increase the pressure for development in locations of historic significance. Examples include King's Cross/St Pancras and the Channel Tunnel Rail Link, Woolwich Arsenal and the Woolwich Crossing, Paddington and Heathrow Express/CrossRail, Deptford/Lewisham and the Docklands Light Railway Extension, Spitalfields and CrossRail, and Borough and the Thameslink/Jubilee Line extension.

Housing

Returns from the 1991 Census show that there are over 2.9 million dwellings in Greater London. The demand for housing in London has remained high despite the overall fall in population. This is explained by the fact that the average household size has fallen consistently since the late 1960s.

Census data show a fall in the average household size in Greater London from 2.41 persons in 1971 to 2.36 in 1991. In inner London the 1991 figure drops to 2.21. This reflects an increase in divorce, one-parent families, greater longevity, and earlier independence and setting up home.

Table 6 shows the percentage breakdown of households by tenure, of owner-occupier, local authority ownership, and private rental, and how this has changed since 1961. The rapid growth of owner-occupation, especially during the 1980s, is particularly significant, and was probably at the expense of both the public and private rented sectors. These changes mirror the Government's policy since the late 1970s to encourage greater owner-occupation through various fiscal measures and the 'right-to-buy' policy.

The decline in average household size in Greater London and the shift to owner-occupation have created a demand for the alteration of historic properties. In areas such as Islington and Spitalfields historic buildings have been brought back in the single family occupation. Elsewhere sub-dividing houses to create flats has adversely affected the interior and exterior of many fine properties. At the same time, a number of small-scale incremental changes in residential areas have had a significant cumulative impact. Frequently these have

Table 6　Housing tenure in Greater London, 1961 - 91

Percentage households in each tenure

	owner-occupied	local authority	private rented*
1961	17	20	64
1971	20	30	49
1981	27	43	30
1991	57	23.5	19.5

*includes housing associations
Source: Census

Fig 48 1930s houses with later alterations

involved permitted development which the local authority has been unable to control effectively, even in many Conservation Areas.

In isolation, effects like these may appear relatively insignificant and their impact difficult to gauge. But over time the picture could look very different. Take, for example, a typical Edwardian suburban street. Twenty years ago it may have consisted of two terraced rows of three-bedroomed houses. During the first half of the 1970s the local planning authority granted permission for the conversion of ten of the houses to flats. The residents who moved in were all car owners who wished to park their cars along the street. To ensure that they had a parking space near their house, some householders paved their front gardens and asked the local highway engineers to install dropped kerbs to make access easier.

In the mid 1980s a cable television company won the franchise to provide cable TV to the Borough and installed cables beneath the pavements along both sides of the street. Unfortunately, the engineering contract did not incorporate adequate safeguards for trees during construction and consequently, three years later, five mature London Planes had to be felled because they had become dangerous. The paving which had become uneven was replaced with tarmac. Not all the residents chose the cable option, seven opting for satellite dishes on the front of their house instead.

Following a spate of burglaries and some effective sales promotion by a security company, alarm boxes appeared on the front of several properties. Many householders replaced the original doors and windows in uPVC. At the same time, a local residents' group lobbied the local authority to implement a package of traffic-calming measures including road narrowing and speed humps following several accidents involving children. Some clumsy workmanship during the painting of white lines resulted in a paint spillage which spread for some distance as vehicles drove through the wet paint. The paint was not cleared up due to an administrative oversight at the town hall.

The effect of these changes, some of which were the responsibility of the planning department, some of the highway

Fig 49 Visual chaos: poorly designed street paving after different phases of work and repair, Barnet

engineers, and some simply the choice of a householder, is a street which has a very different character to that of twenty years ago. Multiply this by the number of streets which fall outside areas subject to any special planning controls and the cumulative impact on the character of London is very dramatic indeed.

A further aspect of the changing character of residential areas is ownership. As former publicly-owned estates have been sold off, the nature of property maintenance has changed, often at the expense of architectural continuity for instance the introduction of different styles of front door, windows, and so on. Conversely, the architectural value of some run-down areas has gradually been restored as perceptions have changed and areas have become fashionable again. This gentrification has been especially prevalent in inner residential areas which are still within reach of the City and West End.

The relationship between housing and available finance is also significant. Currently, arrangements tend to encourage the construction of new dwellings rather than the renewal of existing premises. The exemption from VAT of new build operations is the single most important cause of this imbalance, as it effectively imposes a 17.5% tax on refurbishment schemes. A further contributory factor is the dominance of 'cost per unit' in considering grant aid by bodies such as the Housing Corporation. Additional costs of sensitive restoration of historic or listed properties are likely to exclude such schemes from grant aid, thus shifting the balance in favour of new construction.

London's economy

Industry and commerce
Probably the most significant change in London's economy since the last war is the shift from manufacturing to the service sector, in terms of contributing to Gross Domestic Product (GDP) and in the number of people employed. By 1991 there were 7.6 times more people working in services (85% of employed) than in manufacturing (11%) (LPAC 1994b). The growth in the service sector has fuelled the demand for office space and an associated development boom in each decade since the war. The result has been an increase in the supply of office space in the central area, in suburban town centres, and in new locations like Docklands. A recent survey of land-use change on the Thames-side showed a decline in industrial and commercial uses along the river in 1967-91, with a substantial number being replaced by mixed uses, including offices, shops, restaurants, pubs, cafes, and public buildings (LPAC and London Rivers Association 1992).

Recently the supply of office space in the capital has outstripped demand, with enough in central London to meet present rates of demand for the next ten to fourteen years. Vacancy rates in the early 1990s ran at 17-20% in the City and at 40% in Docklands (LPAC 1992b). The decline of manufacturing industry in London has been matched by a large fall in the amount of industrial land (LPAC 1993a). Although structural changes in the economy have partly been responsible for the fall, the changes introduced by the Use Class Order 1987 and the General Development Order 1988 have had a marked impact in London. This is because many industrial premises have become mixed-use or solely office space. The 1988 General Development Order (GDO) allowed for the change of use to B1 (business) from B2 (general industrial) or B8 (storage and distribution).

Table 4 sets out the main effect of these changes on the historic environment. For example, many of the office redevelopment schemes of the 1980s had a significant negative impact on historic street patterns, buildings, and London's skyline. Canary Wharf is one such example. It has drastically altered the view across central

Fig 50 The Hoover Building, Perivale, Ealing

London from Greenwich and the historic character of the docklands at the Isle of Dogs. Conversely, other changes, notably the creation of the B1 Use Class, have had a mixed effect on the historic environment. In some areas many former historic industrial buildings have been revitalised by being converted for office and other types of use. This has been especially prevalent in central fringe areas such as Euston/Kings Cross, Shoreditch, Spitalfields, and so on. Elsewhere in Clerkenwell, Soho, or Savile Row, for instance, the introduction of the B1 Use Class has displaced traditional small-scale craft industries such as tailoring. The widespread use of legal agreements between local authorities and developers to secure planning advantage has made it possible to secure the use and management of historic buildings and areas which might otherwise have not been viable.

Retailing

Retailing and shopping habits have changed significantly since the war with the introduction of supermarkets in the 1960s, followed by moves towards larger and larger outlets in towns and on purpose-built retail parks. Between 1980 and 1989 over 2.5 million square metres of retail floorspace was approved, under construction, or opened throughout Greater London (LPAC 1991). Almost 50% of this floorspace was located within town centres, while developments in out-of-town and edge-of-centre locations accounted for 42% and 8% respectively. Most of the additions to town centres have been made possible by redevelopment schemes, such as those at Kingston, Ealing, and Wood Green. The impacts on the historic environment have been numerous, both positive and negative:

• loss of some historic buildings and street patterns through redevelopment schemes

• loss of some traditional shopfronts as the chain retailers impose their corporate identity on an area

• restoration of some historic buildings, for instance the Hoover Building, Perivale

- necessary security measures, ranging from shutters, reinforced shopfronts and windows, to policy matters such as securing areas at night, or not having residential accommodation above shops

- the physical decline of some town centres through lack of investment as shops move to edge-of-town and out-of-town locations

The change in the character of town centres is an important issue. Many areas have lost their diversity and interest as they have become dominated by multiple retailers at the expense of smaller independents. This has diminished the character of many districts and drained vitality from local centres. PPG 6 Town centres and retail developments (DoE 1993) emphasises the importance of reversing this trend by promoting positive planning policies which enhance the vitality and viability of town centres.

Tourism and leisure

Tourism

As discussed in chapter 3 London is one of the most important tourist destinations in the world, attracting millions of visitors every year. Table 7 illustrates the generally steady increase in the number of visitors between 1982 and 1987. The number of domestic visitors fell off sharply in the late 80s and early 90s, which presumably reflected the depressed state of the economy. The slight reduction in overseas visitors during the early 1990s is probably linked to concern about possible terrorism in the UK following the Gulf War.

London's historic properties all attract substantial numbers of visitors. For example, British Tourist Authority and London Tourist Board data show that Westminster Abbey, the Tower of London, and St Paul's Cathedral all received more than two million visitors in 1993. Some attractions, however, received fewer visitors

Fig 51 Tourists outside Buckingham Palace

in 1993 than they did in 1977. For example the number of tourists visiting the Tower dropped from 3.1 million to 2.3 million, and to Hampton Court Palace from 717,000 to 600,000. The BTA suggests that these reductions are due partly to pricing policies and partly to the greater range of attractions on offer in London. The critical issue appears to be how to manage visitor numbers in order to

Table 7 Visits to London (millions) 1982 – 92

year	overseas	domestic
1982	7.1	13
1983	7.6	15
1984	8.4	13
1985	9 1	14
1986	8.2	13
1987	9.3	15
1988	9.1	12
1989	9.9	(9)
1990	10.3	(7)
1991	9.2	(6.5)
1992	10	(7.0)

Source: London Tourist Board and Convention Bureau
Note: ( ) = new series

get the right balance between enough visitors to generate income for upkeep and to protect sensitive historic sites from damage caused by the volume of people. The Royal Parks Review gives evidence that the balance may be tipping unfavourably towards the latter in historic areas which are not subject to pricing controls; 'St James's and Green Parks lie at the historic heart of the nation, the centre of palaces and pomp, of politics and power.... St James's and Green Parks are different in style but both are hugely popular. Visitor counts taken during the market research in August and October 1992 suggest about 15 million visits a year. They suffer from a multitude of feet and, in the case of St James's, too many birds. Both show signs of physical exhaustion; care and money will be required to ensure their continuing health and beauty' (DNH 1993)

Conversely, in other locations visitor pressure has stimulated the investment of care and money in historic attractions advocated by the Royal Parks Review Group. The new Jewel Room at the Tower of London, the environmental improvements in Regent's Street and Leicester Square, and the restoration of Avenue Gardens in Regent's Park are evidence of this trend. Elsewhere there has not been enough recognition of those elements which make London distinctive or unique for the visitor. For instance, the loss of traditional red telephone kiosks and the fragmentation of London Buses, with the consequent loss of their distinctive red livery and strictly controlled advertising, have undermined the visual cohesion which once characterised London and gave it a distinctive international image.

Leisure

PPG 17 *Sport and Recreation* (DoE 1991a) states that in 1986 there were 21 million adults in Great Britain regularly taking part in indoor or outdoor sport, an increase of 7% since 1977, and that many more enjoy the informal recreational opportunities offered by open space in the countryside. In a city the size of London, the increased demand for sport and recreation facilities obviously places extra pressure on open space. The popularity of golf illustrates one potential problem in that historic landscapes are very attractive locations for new golf courses because they provide an instant backdrop. Recent research undertaken by LPAC (1993c) on landscape change in London's Green Belt and metropolitan open land illustrates this point. The parkland and common land landscapes in the case study areas witnessed a decline in total area, with golf courses identified as one of the reasons for the decline and the resulting change in character. The development of a golf course within Osterley Park is cited as an example.

Data compiled by the National Playing Fields Association show that the use of approximately 1.5% of the total national stock of playing fields has changed since 1989. In London, numerous local authority school playing fields have been sold off for development, eroding the open setting of parts of London and increasing the pressure for recreation on those open areas which remain.

Agriculture

Significant parts of Greater London remain in agricultural use because of the success of the Green Belt and Metropolitan Open Land designations in preventing wholesale loss to development. Nevertheless, recent research has shown that agricultural land in Greater London has changed considerably since 1949 (LPAC 1993c). For example, there has been a gradual increase in average field size as farmers have tried to make agricultural holdings more productive. Also, the overall character of the open land has been altered by uses which are deemed acceptable or have been permitted in the Green Belt, including urban development for instance residential, industrial, and commercial development, as well as an increase in schools and car parks, transport routes, and rural development, including the conversion of glasshouses and farm buildings to commercial and industrial uses, active mineral workings, and disturbed land.

The LPAC report concludes that, while the Green Belt and Metropolitan Open Land have remained relatively unaffected by development and land-use change which is incompatible with these designations, landscape character has changed significantly and landscape quality has often deteriorated.

Technological change

The wider impact of technological change on the shape on London should also not be underestimated. It is interesting to reflect, for example, that only in relatively recent times have we been able to use cash machines, receive television programmes through a cable or satellite dish, and travel on electric trains. These technological advances have generated alterations to the urban environment to accommodate them, and many have had a negative impact in important historic streets and areas. Two notable examples are the proliferation of

Fig 52 The Pumping Station, Green Lanes, Hackney

satellite dishes and other communications equipment on the exterior of buildings, and the damage to paving stones, kerbs, and tree roots caused by cable-laying along pavements. However, technological advances may make further damage less likely. Developments in information technology mean that underground cabling may become unnecessary, although new developments may still affect the historic environment.

Changes in the public sector

The public sector has changed considerably in the last ten to fifteen years. In London this has been most evident in local government with the removal of one tier of government, the GLC, and the redistribution of its functions to the London Boroughs and various other agencies. Over the same period, public expenditure has been reduced, and, as a consequence, government, local authorities, and other public organisations, such as health authorities, have had to raise income from other sources, with one of the most profitable being the disposal of assets such as land and buildings. British Rail has also worked on realising the value of its land and property assets across the capital. Privatisation of the utilities has resulted in the disposal of excess assets as new companies invest in new technology and diversify their activities.

Recent research by English Heritage (1995) confirms the uncertainty surrounding many public buildings. About a quarter of the buildings on the *Register of Buildings at Risk in Greater London* (EH 1994), a schedule of listed buildings deemed to be 'at risk' from neglect or dilapidation, are owned, or have recently been disposed of, by public bodies. Restructuring of the public sector, including local government, the Ministry of Defence, the Health Service, and the privatisation of transport and utilities has meant that town halls, libraries, hospitals, schools, military barracks, fire stations, and railway property, designed for special social needs and once thought permanent, are becoming increasingly redundant and disused. For those public agencies which are not able to dispose of buildings, the prospect for productive reuse in the short term appears bleak because of the constraints on expenditure.

Financial constraints in the public sector have also led to a reduction in specialist staff in some boroughs who deal with applications for listed buildings consent , and in particular their implementation on site. This is crucial at a time when many developers do not retain a specialist architect to supervise on site, even if they obtain planning permission or listed building consent.

Property ownership

Using modern materials to reduce maintenance costs has had a negative impact on many important buildings. For example, pension funds now own many historic properties. They prefer repair and conservation materials and techniques which will minimise maintenance, and often tend to over-restore in order to reduce maintenance liability. They have frequently resisted using upper floors above shops in historic buildings or areas for accommodation or office use, giving security as a reason, but probably also with lease and tenancy complications in mind. Consequently many shopping and commercial areas are dead at night because people are excluded from using them.

Growth of the conservation movement

The conservation movement has helped to create an impressive body of conservation legislation shaping the fabric of cities we see today. The pressures to use land and buildings thought worthy of preservation have enabled the growth of a well-informed, well-organised, and effective movement for protecting these assets. In London, the Survey of London and the special conservation powers vested first in the London County Council, then in the GLC, and now in the London Region of English Heritage bear testimony to the success of the movement. The history of planning in London is littered by battles between conservationists, planners, and developers, some of which the conservation movement have won, for instance at Covent Garden, Piccadilly Circus, Spitalfields, and the Oxo buildings, and some have been lost, for instance the Firestone Building, Globe House, and the Euston Arch. Much of London's historic environment which survives today only does so because of the determined efforts of the conservation movement.

The implications for conservation in London

Many land-use changes have had and continue to have a negative impact on the historic environment. For example, the extent to which many of London's important public buildings have become redundant, or face the threat of redundancy, is of concern because of their contribution to the overall character and quality of London. However, the cumulative impact of the gradual erosion of quality, character, and setting emerges as a concern when considering the state of the historic environment, but it is difficult to quantify. A glance at the *Register of Buildings at Risk in Greater London* provides some useful pointers. Appendix 3 gives information regarding the distribution of buildings at risk across the capital.

There are many reasons why so many buildings on the Register face an uncertain future, yet it seems reasonable to conclude that a sizeable proportion are the physical manifestation of some of the changes identified in Table 4. Another possible explanation is provided by Figure 52 which shows the percentage of the total number of buildings at risk by Borough. The Boroughs with more than 5% of the total of buildings at risk in London are concentrated in the east and inner areas, Tower Hamlets, Hackney, and Islington. All of these Boroughs have relatively high numbers of listed buildings and it is perhaps not surprising, therefore, that the percentage of these at risk is relatively high suggesting a link between buildings prone to neglect and dilapidation, and inner-city

Fig 53 The Hotel Splendide, Mornington Crescent, Camden

areas of acute social and economic stress. To test this hypothesis, we compared the buildings at risk data with the Department of the Environment's *Index of local Conditions* (see Table 8).

Four of the five Boroughs identified by the DOE as the most deprived in London also have relatively high concentrations of listed buildings at risk, while many of the least deprived Boroughs have low concentrations. There seems to be a direct link between social and economic stress and the problem of historic buildings amd areas at risk.

Concentrations of buildings at risk highlight areas which have suffered from

Table 8 Comparison of index of local conditions and Buildings at Risk

borough	local condition rank	% of total no Buildings at Risk in London
Newham	1	1.7
Southwark	2	9.5
Hackney	3	13.9
Islington	4	7.1
Tower Hamlets	5	18.1
Lambeth	6	4.7
Haringey	7	1.6
Lewisham	8	0.8
Greenwich	9	2.6
Camden	10	7.3
H'smith &	11	0.4
Bark.& Dag.	12	0
Ken.& Chelsea	13	3.7
Waltham Forest	14	1.2
Wandsworth	15	3.0
Westminster	16	6.0
Brent	17	1.0
Ealing	18	0.3
City	19	1.7
Enfield	20	1.5
Hounslow	21	1.7
Merton	22	1.0
Redbridge	23	1.5
Kingston	24	0.6
Croydon	25	0.7
Barnet	26	1.1
Hillingdon	27	1.2
Havering	28	1.2
Richmond	29	1.1
Bexley	30	1.2
Sutton	31	0.6
Harrow	32	0.2
Bromley	33	1.3
Fulham	-	-

Fig 54 High concentrations of buildings at risk

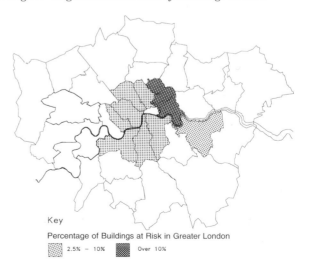

Key

Percentage of Buildings at Risk in Greater London

2.5% – 10%   Over 10%

economic and social decline over many years. The buildings themselves will be in a poor state of repair and therefore likely to be a blight on their surroundings, especially if the building is not within a Conservation Area. However, the reverse is probably also true where an area in decline drags individual buildings down with it. Figure 4 shows high concentrations of buildings at risk in the Boroughs on the eastern side of London and in some inner areas. This distribution tends to confirm that there is a link between lack of investment and a failure to protect environmental quality and conserve the historic environment. The concentration of public and private investment to the west of London and resulting east-west imbalance has had a largely negative impact on the historic environment of inner and east London. Clearly, as policies pay more attention to the Thames Gateway, there will be opportunities to change the imbalance.

Conclusions

The analysis of the effects of land-use trends on the historic environment confirms the widely-held view that, despite the recognition of its value, the character and quality of London's historic environment is being eroded, in particular in inner and east London. Research and statistical data highlight several factors which appear to have contributed to this, notably increased levels of traffic and congestion, disposal of historic public buildings, increased visitor pressure on historic attractions, and the changing character of much of the open land around London. The analysis also suggests a positive correlation between neglect of the historic environment and more general physical, social, and economic malaise.

The situation, however, is far from being entirely negative. First, and most importantly, an impressive body of conservation legislation has been put in place in response to heightened public awareness of the damage inflicted on the historic environment. There is substantial evidence that this is working well, although the reluctance of many local authorities to use their statutory powers to repair buildings at risk, for instance, has inhibited progress. General planning legislation too has helped to secure the productive use of buildings through, for example, planning agreements. In addition no attempt has been made in Figure 54 to distinguish between those changes which may be temporary or transitional and those which are long-term and permanent. Sites may often lie derelict, vacant, and deteriorating for long periods even though there may be general agreement that the eventual repair of historic buildings, and regeneration of their areas, will eventually take place, at Kings Cross or Woolwich Arsenal for instance. There is a pressing need to manage redundancy, disposal, and reuse arising from structural economic change more effectively and smoothly to avoid the deterioration of buildings and a decrease in their asset value .

This same public awareness has sparked an influential conservation movement that has helped to secure the protection of many elements of the historic environment which would otherwise have been lost through redevelopment. Also, some land-use trends, such as the demand for office space in converted historic buildings, have enhanced the vitality and viability of many parts of London.

Fig 55 The Granary and gasholders at King's Cross, Camden

5 The policy context for conservation

In this chapter the policy context is examined in which strategic guidance on the conservation of London's historic environment must be considered. It shows that there is not only widespread recognition of the value of conservation but also strong support for it in policy and guidance formulated internationally, in Europe, and by the UK Government.

International policies

Agenda 21 has been described as the most significant outcome of the 1992 Earth Summit in Rio de Janeiro. Among its issues, chapter 7 on 'Sustainable human settlements' argues for better management of towns and cities, because they provide the most environmentally efficient form of human settlement. It states that towns and cities must be managed to sustain productivity, improve living conditions, and manage resources sustainably (Local Government Management Board 1993). Conservation can help to meet these objectives.

European policies

In the absence of any clear statement of European policy, the Commission of the European Communities' Green Paper on the urban environment (Commission of the European Communities 1990) indicates the approach that Member States should adopt. This states that 'the historical centres of European cities represent an important link with the city's past culture and heritage. In a world increasingly dominated by international styles of architecture and building technology, historical centres provide a unique sense of place which differentiates one town from another .... Interest in protecting a city's historical character is therefore not restricted to that city's citizens'.

The Green Paper goes on to describe some of the pressures which have resulted in the destruction of much of the historical fabric of our cities, including large-scale demolition and renewal, dereliction of inner-city, residential, and industrial areas, and road development and pollution from motor vehicles. The Green Paper advocates more substantial financing to conserve historic buildings and 'areas of European significance', and a Community-wide recognition of the historic and cultural value of individual buildings and parts of urban areas.

National policies

Successive UK governments have placed great importance on conserving the nation's heritage. The Ancient Monuments Act of 1893 was the first State action to secure the conservation of historic buildings and monuments, and was a response to mounting pressures from voluntary organisations, such as the Society for the Preservation of Ancient Monuments and the National Trust for Places of Historic Interest or Natural Beauty, founded in 1877 and 1895 respectively.

A formal procedure for listing buildings of special architectural or historic interest was introduced by the Town and Country Planning Act 1944, later part of the Town and Country Planning Act of 1947 which, by nationalising the right to develop land or change the use of buildings, allowed much greater control over historic buildings. Central to the concept of listing is that all protected buildings need listed building consent where any proposed change to them would affect their character as a building of special architectural or historic interest. The listing procedure remains very similar today and provides the best known and understood form of protection for historic buildings. The Civic Amenities Act of 1967 highlighted the need to protect areas of architectural or historic interest, as opposed to individual buildings. It empowered local authorities to designate Conservation Areas, and to date over 8000 Conservation Areas have been designated in England and Wales, of which some 800 are in Greater London. The Town and Country Planning (Amendment) Act 1972 gave statutory meaning to Conservation Areas, by enabling local authorities to control the demolition of unlisted buildings in a Conservation Area, and the Secretary of State, on the advice of English Heritage, was empowered to make available grants or loans for 'outstanding' Conservation Areas.

While the legislative machinery for conserving the historic environment has served the country very well, there has been a recent shift in emphasis towards a more holistic view of the environment, and a recognition of the need to integrate policies. 'Sustainable development' is the term frequently used to express this approach. It has many definitions, but its meaning is encapsulated very well in the 1990 UK Environment White Paper *This common inheritance* (DoE): 'sustainable development ...... means living on the earth's income rather than eroding its capital. It means keeping the consumption of renewable natural resources within the limits of their replenishment. It means handing down to successive generations not only man-made wealth (such as buildings, roads and railways) but also natural wealth, such as clean and adequate water supplies, good arable land, a wealth of wildlife and ample forests'.

The White Paper confirmed the Government's commitment to sustainable development, and also made it very clear that conserving the historic environment is central to achieving the objectives of sustainable development and that the Government gives it high priority. 'Everyone wants to protect the best of urban and rural environments, so that we can pass on to our children what we value

most about our own heritage'. It also summarises the Government's policy towards the conservation of the historic environment as looking after properties in Government care, promoting enjoyment and understanding of the heritage, encouraging private-sector efforts and making financial assistance available, identifying and recording the best of our heritage, and ensuring that the legislative system properly protects and preserves it.

The UK's strategy for sustainable development (DOE 1994b) emphasises reusing and redeveloping land and buildings, and notes the establishment of a new body in 1993, English Partnerships, to promote the reclamation and development of vacant and derelict land and buildings, particularly in urban areas. The strategy also stated that 'the built heritage comprises remains of past human settlements, religion, industry and land use. It includes ancient monuments, archaeological sites, historical buildings and gardens, industrial remains and other landscape features of historic interest. For the prehistoric and many other historic periods, such remains form the only source of evidence for understanding the UK's past. It is, therefore, important that historically and aesthetically important monuments, buildings, sites and landscapes are maintained and protected for future generations. Failure to do so would result in irreversible loss of the nation's heritage'.

The Government's support for conservation, as a principle of sustainable development, is reflected in its Planning Policy Guidance Notes (PPGs). PPG 12 *Development plans and regional planning guidance* (DoE 1992b) takes the lead by stating that plans 'should take environmental considerations comprehensively and consistently into account'. It defines environmental considerations very broadly, but stresses that plans should give high priority to conserving the built and archaeological heritage, to good design in new development, and to encouraging the arts. Conservation of the historic environment also finds expression in many of the topic-based PPGs issued by the Department of the Environment. Most notable amongst these are PPG 15 *Planning and the historic environment* (1994c) and paragraph 20 of PPG 4 *Industrial development and small firms* (1992a). PPG 6 *Town centres and retail development* (1993), gives further support for stronger conservation policy. It states that the Government's aim is to sustain or enhance the vitality and viability of town centres, an objective compatible with sustainable development. As noted in chapter 3, the conservation of historic landmark buildings can play a crucial role in the revival of town centres.

English Heritage, in association with English Nature and the Countryside Commission, has published guidance on how conservation issues should be addressed in strategic plans, ie regional strategies and structure plans (Countryside Commission, English Heritage, and English Nature, 1993). One of the purposes of this is to give advice on the meaning of sustainable development and ways of achieving it, and the integration of different strands of conservation. It emphasises key sustainability principles for conservation:

• environmental capacity and thresholds, ie judging whether environmental resources are able or not to accept demands without irreversible or otherwise unacceptable loss or damage

• demand management, ie modifying future development needs by managing current demand

Regional policy context

The Government's Regional planning guidance for the south east (March 1994) gives the regional framework for London's strategic planning guidance. It defines a number of principles which are intended to govern the development of the region.

These indicate that '...... the fullest possible use should be made of opportunities for redevelopment and recycling of urban land. The aim should be not only to secure development and urban regeneration, but also to improve the urban environment and reduce the need to take greenfield sites for development ...' and '... development should respect the region's valuable environmental features and avoid the wasteful use of land and other natural resources. Firm protection will be maintained over .... the built heritage ....'.

Regional guidance also stresses that local authorities should approach the planning, environmental, and traffic management of historic towns (including London) with particular care.

Policies for London

London has been in the vanguard of the conservation movement since its first systematic development in the late nineteenth century. It contains the highest concentration of buildings thought worthy of preservation, and those buildings have been constantly threatened by rival pressures for the use of urban land. In its pioneering years, the development of conservation was closely linked to a growth in civic consciousness, and to the development of London's municipal government. Shortly after its establishment in 1887 the London County Council involved itself in conservation and in 1899 it set up its own register of historic buildings. Abercrombie's *County of London Plan* (1943) emphasised the reconstruction of London following the war, and also recognised the need for strong conservation policies. 'London possesses a great wealth of buildings of historic interest and of outstanding architectural merit. These, in a large measure, give to the metropolis its external character and interest, and reveal its evolution and traditions. A London denuded of these buildings would be vastly poorer. The destruction of so many buildings of this character during the war and the possible destruction of others, makes it more than ever a duty to preserve, as far as practicable, those remaining'. However, the *Greater London Plan* of 1944 paid very little attention to conserving London's historic environment, and concentrated on, among other things, decanting London's population into new satellite towns.

The need for strong conservation policies was brought back into sharp focus by the Greater London Council's 1976 Greater London Development Plan (GLDP). This was in part a reflection of the 'over-enthusiastic' redevelopment that occurred after the war and during the 1960s. The GLDP sought to initiate 'a more vigorous and comprehensive policy for the conservation of the features that gives London its distinctive character'. It defined 'Areas of Special Character', covering precincts and areas that the Council considered to be important to the city. The Plan also laid down a set of principles which Boroughs were expected to follow when considering planning applications for high buildings.

Strategic guidance for London (RPG 3, DoE 1989b) was published by the Secretary of State for the Environment to help London Boroughs prepare their Unitary Development Plans. Among other objectives it sought to contribute to the revitalisation of the older urban areas, maintain the vitality and character of established town centres, sustain and improve the amenity of residential areas, and give high priority to the environment by preserving fine views and Conservation Areas. Specific guidance is given on three issues, conservation of the built environment, important views, and archaeology.

On the conservation of the built environment RPG 3 referred to the Government's policies in DOE Circular 8/87: *Historic buildings and Conservation Areas* (now superseded by PPG 15). On the matter of important views, RPG 3 indicated that strategic views of St Paul's Cathedral and the Palace of Westminster, which are of historic importance, must be protected from obtrusive development. Supplementary guidance on this issue was published in November 1991, and identified ten strategic views that should be afforded protection, Primrose Hill to St Paul's Cathedral, Primrose Hill to the Palace of Westminster, Parliament Hill to St Paul's Cathedral, Parliament Hill to the Palace of Westminster, Kenwood to St Paul's Cathedral, Alexandra Palace to St Paul's Cathedral, Greenwich Park to St Paul's Cathedral, Blackheath Point to St Paul's Cathedral, Richmond Park (King Henry VIII's Mound) to St Paul's Cathedral, and Westminster Pier to St Paul's Cathedral.

Advice on strategic planning guidance for London (LPAC 1994a) identifies the River Thames as London's most important visual element and recommends that all proposals for development affecting it should be appropriate to the unique character and quality of the river, and should protect strategic and local views. On archaeology, the Guidance indicates that Boroughs should preserve their ancient monuments and their settings.

Conclusions

Two main conclusions can be drawn from this review of the policy context. The first is that there is not only widespread recognition of the value of conservation, but also strong support for it in existing policies formulated internationally, in Europe, and by the UK Government. Conservation of the built environment is now a fundamental tenet in the move towards sustainable development. In the light of this it is clear that current strategic policy for the conservation and enhancement of London's historic environment needs expanding and reinforcing. At present it is divorced from wider urban concerns and does not carry the same weight as the other policy areas.

6 Conclusions and recommendations

Conclusions

This study defines strategic planning policy options for 1996 to 2010, seeking to integrate conservation, enhancement, and positive use of London's historic environment with evolving patterns of regeneration and development in the capital. Such a study was felt to be necessary because of increasing concern that the capital's historic environment continues to be under threat from inappropriate development and other adverse change. Both commissioning agencies, English Heritage and LPAC, believe this has serious implications, particularly in detracting from the four-fold vision for London put forward in LPAC's advice on strategic planning guidance for London (LPAC 1994a).

The study defines London's rich historic environment by combining a review of planning designations and definitions with a description of the evolution of the capital. This has highlighted three important issues, of which the first is the consistency of the interpretation and application of conservation designations and definitions by all the Boroughs. For example, large parts of the London suburbs do not achieve adequate recognition, like much of the open land on the eastern and western edges of the city.

The second issue relates to London's historic environment being more than the sum of its parts. There is an inherent danger in only considering the historic environment as being those parts of Greater London which have achieved some form of recognition, ie a designation or definition. London has a richness and diversity, not necessarily apparent from the designations and definitions established for planning purposes.

London's evolution also highlights the third issue. There is a recurring theme.

Some areas have undergone a sustained improvement, while elsewhere there has been a gradual erosion of the quality and character of London's historic environment. The conclusion drawn is that existing systems of control are not enough to regulate some of the damaging changes which are occurring, in particular in relation to alterations to highways and domestic buildings in Conservation Areas, and the need to manage the redundancy and disposal of major historic buildings and sites more effectively.

Having defined the historic environment, the study demonstrates the value of conserving London's historic environment from three perspectives, environmental, social, and economic. Value goes well beyond the aesthetic and spiritual importance of protecting historic buildings, monuments, and spaces, crucial though these are. Conservation is an opportunity to give practical expression to sustainability principles and contributes to the economic well-being of London and the nation. Conserving the historic environment also retains a sense of place and identity, and maintains balanced, harmonious communities and a diverse mix of uses.

The analysis of the effects of land-use trends on the historic environment confirms the widely-held view that, despite the recognition of its value, the character and quality of London's historic environment is under threat in several areas. Research and statistical data highlight factors which have contributed to this erosion, notably increased levels of traffic and congestion, disposal of historic public sector assets in land and property, increased visitor pressure on historic attractions, and the changing character of the open land around London. The analysis also suggests a positive correlation between neglect of the historic environment and a more general physical, social, and economic malaise.

The situation, however, is not all negative. First, and most importantly, an impressive body of conservation legislation has been put in place in response to heightened public awareness of the damage inflicted on the historic environment. In some areas the quality of new buildings has improved to take account of their wider historic architectural and townscape context. General planning legislation too has helped secure the productive use of buildings through, for example, planning agreements and a more proactive approach to regeneration and the economic reuse of historic buildings.

This same public awareness has sparked an influential conservation movement that has helped to secure the protection of many elements of the historic environment which would otherwise have been lost through redevelopment. Also, some land-use trends, such as the demand for office space in converted historic buildings, have enhanced the vitality and viability of many parts of London.

Chapter 5 outlines the policy context in which strategic guidance on the conservation of London's historic environment must be considered. Two main conclusions may be drawn. The first is that there is not only widespread recognition of the value of conservation, but also strong support for it in policy formulated internationally, in Europe, and by the UK Government. Conservation is now a fundamental tenet in the move towards sustainable development. On this basis, we feel that current strategic policy for the conservation and enhancement of London's historic environment is inadequate, divorced from wider urban concerns and falls short of current policy expectations.

Recommendations

Conserving London's historic environment is of real value. It is fundamental to the capital's future prosperity and its role as a world city. We recommend six policy initiatives to realise this potential. These should be seen as part of a single process of strategic planning and environmental management with the aim of securing a high-quality built environment which protects and enhances London's unique character. The main agencies responsible for implementation are identified in each case.

Recommendation 1:
Promote London's historic framework as a feature of national and international importance

The revised version, of *Advice on strategic planning guidance* for London (LPAC 1994a) should integrate the conservation of London's historic environment with other aspects of strategic policy. It should incorporate a map of the historic framework, based on the version reproduced below, and set out the requirement for policies to conserve buildings, monuments, spaces, artefacts, and views which give London its unique character.

Particular attention should be paid to aspects of the historic environment which warrant enhanced protection, including the distinctive towns, villages, and suburbs, and views of important national and local landmarks not currently

protected by strategic guidance, eg the Tower of London, London Bridge, Buckingham Palace and the Mall, St Pancras Station, Whitehall and the River Thames. The map of the historic framework and supporting policies for strategic guidance should be prepared jointly by English Heritage, LPAC, and the Department of the Environment.

Implementation of this recommendation would:

• promote a greater awareness of the extent of London's historic environment

• provide a policy framework for the effective management of London's historic environment and inform development control and the review of UDPs

• encourage full use of all existing measures for the preservation and enhancement of the historic environment and explore the need for new measures

Fig 56 Map of the historic environment

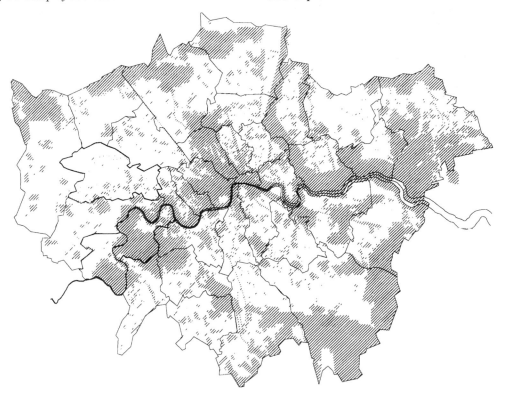

Fig 57 St Andrew's Wharf, Shad Thames, Southwark

- emphasise the relationship between the component parts of the historic environment and promote a multi-disciplinary approach to conservation

- expand the focus of conservation from individual buildings and structures to areas and to the wider setting of London's historic environment

- complement the environmental framework in LPAC's 1994 *Advice on Strategic Planning Guidance for London*

Agencies responsible for implementation:

LPAC/English Heritage: preparation of supplementary planning advice on conservation

Department of the Environment/ Government Office for London: preparation of strategic planning guidance for London

London Boroughs: development control and review of UDPs

Recommendation 2:

Promote conservation as a focus for urban regeneration, particularly in inner and east London, the Lea Valley and Thames Gateway, and in key strategic locations such as King's Cross/St Pancras, Paddington, Battersea Power Station, Spitalfields, Park Royal, North Southwark, and Woolwich Arsenal.

Conservation can act as an important catalyst for urban regeneration. Investment in conservation, whether through Conservation Area partnerships, renovation of buildings at risk (also see recommendation 3), or other spending initiatives should be targeted at the Regeneration Areas defined in *Advice on Strategic Planning Guidance for London* (LPAC 1994a). The map below shows the Regeneration Areas and provides a framework for prioritising expenditure.

Implementation of this recommendation would:

• highlight the central role of conservation in the regeneration of inner and east London, the Lea Valley and the Thames Gateway

• maximise the opportunities for investment in the historic fabric through enabling development and investment in public transport infrastructure

• reinforce the existing and proposed policy initiatives to enhance the vitality and viability of town centres

• inform the targeting of the Single Regeneration Budget for London

• promote a strategy for dynamic, mixed-use town centres co-ordinated by town centre managers

• provide a coherent planning framework for conservation-based area regeneration

Agencies responsible for implementation:

LPAC/English Heritage: Preparation of supplementary planning advice on conservation.
Department of the Environment/Government Office for London: Preparation of strategic planning guidance for London, targeting of resources to areas of need
English Heritage: Prioritise expenditure on conservation
English Partnerships: Ensure grant money for regeneration is targeted at conservation-based projects

Fig 58 Map of regeneration areas

LPAC Regeneration Area

Recommendation 3:
Secure a viable future for historic buildings and areas at risk

Returning buildings and areas at risk to a viable and appropriate use should be a high priority as a catalyst for area-wide regeneration. It should be seen as investment in the long-term future of an area and an indication of confidence.

English Heritage has prepared a gazetteer of redundant public buildings which includes examples of buildings successfully recycled to productive uses. It has also taken the lead in adopting a programme of action to tackle the problem, concentrating on Grade I and II* buildings and buildings in public ownership. Each London Borough needs to devise a strategy to address the problem as an integral part of economic development and area-based regeneration, involving a mixture of statutory action, incentives, and voluntary action. We recommend the following criteria for defining buildings with a high priority for action:

• Buildings in public ownership

• Vacant listed buildings in poor condition

• Landmark buildings of local significance

• Neglected and decaying historic areas including parks, gardens, and cemeteries

• Buildings which would make a significant contribution to area-wide regeneration

• Where a public institutional use can be matched with an important vacant historic building

Implementation of this recommendation would:

• focus effort, attention, and resources on finding new uses for dilapidated and neglected buildings

• provide a catalyst for area-wide regeneration

• inform the targeting of the Single Regeneration Budget for London

• develop a more effective strategy for the management of the disposal of redundant buildings and sites

• enhance the townscape of local areas currently blighted by buildings at risk

• retain buildings which help to create local identity in many of London's town centres

Agencies responsible for implementation:

English Heritage: Disseminate information about buildings at risk and prioritise funds in accordance with the recommended criteria
London Boroughs: Give priority to the buildings at risk in planning policy, implementation, and enforcement
Department of the Environment/ Government Office for London/English Partnerships/English Heritage: Devise a more effective strategy for managing the disposal of redundant historic buildings including agencies to oversee the long-term development of complex sites

Fig 59 A building at risk in Ashfield Street, Tower Hamlets

Recommendation 4:
Promote an integrated transport and land-use planning policy

Promoting an integrated transport and land-use planning policy would encourage further expansion and use of public transport, improve access, and reduce the impact of traffic on the historic environment. This should be given a high priority. PPG 13 *Transport* is a blueprint for transport policy and it should be taken up in London as a matter of urgency if further erosion of the quality and character of the historic environment is to be avoided.

The following action is recommended:

• Integrate transport and land-use planning policies to reduce dependence on the private car, maximise the efficiency and effectiveness of public transport, and reduce travelling between home and work by supporting the development of mixed-use urban villages

• Better co-ordination between new transport infrastructure and the wider urban design and land-use context to ensure maximum advantage for the historic environment from public and private investment

• Review parking provisions, controls, and parking standards for new development to reduce commuting by private car and minimise the impact of traffic on the historic environment

• Close co-operation at a national level between English Heritage and the highways and traffic agencies, and at a local level within local authorities, to reconcile highway works, traffic calming, and other traffic-related measures with the character and appearance of historic areas. This could take the form of regular liaison meetings and joint guidance and advice.

Fig 60 Traffic in central London

Implementation of this recommendation would:

• help to reduce the impact of traffic on London's historic environment

• encourage cooperation and communication in common language between those involved in transport planning

• improve the standard of design and implementation of highway works

Agencies responsible for implementation:

English Heritage/Civic Trust/English Historic Towns Forum: Promote schemes which demonstrate good design practice in accordance with *Traffic measures in historic towns*
English Heritage/Department of Transport/Highways Agency: Convene regular liaison meetings with all agencies involved in transport in London to address issues affecting the historic environment
London Boroughs: Co-ordination of land-use and transport planning as part of development control process. Develop an integrated multi-disciplinary approach to transport and conservation within departmental structures.

Recommendation 5:

Promote joint boroughs initiative to highlight conservation within a London-wide state of the environment audit

The Government has published a Good Practice Guide on the environmental appraisal of development plans. This guide emphasises characterising the environment through an assessment of environment stock (defined as those elements of the environment which can be identified and measured). The Boroughs should work together to prepare a London-wide audit of the historic environment. The audit should be an integral part both of the appraisal of UDPs and strategic guidance and cover the following points:

Recording the condition of the historic environment

Many London Boroughs have published or are preparing state of the environment reports. These are an opportunity to record the condition of the historic environment and should form the basis for Conservation Area statements which provide an integrated approach to townscape management. Particular consideration should be given to the appropriate designation of areas which are often overlooked as part of the historic environment, eg suburban centres, cemeteries and churchyards, hospital complexes, historic parks and landscapes, and inter-war and post-war housing estates. This study provides a London-wide framework which the Boroughs may choose to use as a reference point for such an exercise.

English Heritage is carrying out a review of Conservation Area designations across London with a view to ensuring greater consistency. Research is underway on suburban housing to ensure that the most significant areas are protected adequately.

Condition of the local historic environment: some suggested key indicators

Qualitative

- commentary on the Borough's historic character

- description of historic landmarks

- description of the nature and extent of the setting of the historic environment

- description of factors which have eroded the historic fabric eg insensitive highway works and loss of traditional shopfronts

Quantitative

- number of designated areas

- criteria for designation

- number of listed buildings

- percentage of listed buildings at risk

- number of vacant historic properties

- number of listed building consents approved/refused by building type or location, as a measure of pressure for change

- production of local lists and local inventories of parks, gardens, or other land of historic interest

- identification of the nature and extent of areas where the historic environment has been eroded

- number of historic properties returned to productive use by building type and location

Setting environmental targets for the historic environment

Local authorities should set environmental targets for the historic environment, which might include :

• consistent interpretation and application of criteria for conservation designations and definition within the Borough and with adjacent Boroughs/districts around London

• a conservation input in all relevant decisions taken by the authority, especially those outside the planning department

• an effective balance of mixed uses of buildings to reinforce the character and function of local historic centres

• the reinstatement of the historic character of areas where overall quality or individual features have been eroded

• reducing the number of listed buildings at risk to a minimal percentage of the total stock within two years

• defining the environmental capacity of key tourist attractions and sites to ensure sustainable future development

• undertaking regular street audits to rationalise street furniture, reduce clutter, and remove superfluous or redundant signs in accordance with the advice set out in PPG15

Providing adequate planning policy coverage

The condition of, and environmental targets for, the historic environment should be fully reflected in planning policy in UDPs.

Appraisal of policies

All land-use related policies of the Borough should be appraised for their impact on the historic environment. The appraisal should cover the UDP and other policy statements such as the Transport Policy Programme (TPP)

Implementation of this recommendation would:

• establish a comprehensive inventory of London's historic resource against which plans, policies, programmes, and development projects can be assessed

• provide a key input to the London state of the environment report

• facilitate the application of sustainability principles as part of the UDPs on environmental capacity and thresholds, and demand management

Agencies responsible for implementation:

London Boroughs/LPAC: organise and undertake London-wide audit
Local amenity groups/English Heritage: provide information for the audit

Fig 61 Street furniture clutter, Lamb's Conduit Street, Camden

Recommendation 6:
Encourage effective management of London's historic environment

Conservation should be fully integrated with all other plan policies at UDP stage as an holistic approach to the management of change. It needs to permeate thinking at all levels of the planning process. Once an integrated policy base has been secured, effective implementation can only be achieved through efficient integrated management at a local level. This is a fundamental precursor of urban quality.

Local authorities should reassess their departmental management structures to achieve integrated, high-quality, conservation-based decision making. It is of paramount importance that, in future, highway planning, for instance, is carried out within a wider conservation-based framework so that decisions are not simply traffic-led but take full account of the total environmental impact.

Adequate resources are essential for the better management of the historic environment. English Heritage's Conservation Area Partnership programme, and the advent of lottery funding for heritage-based projects, offer an unprecedented opportunity.

The following action is recommended:

- an holistic approach to conservation involving integrated corporate policy-making at local level and, where necessary, departmental restructuring to co-ordinate the management of change within a clear conservation-based strategy

- effective care and management of the historic environment based on a conservation audit by each local authority leading to a clear, phased conservation management strategy

- adequate resources to be employed to manage the historic environment at a local level and to maximise its economic, social, and environmental potential

- preparation of statements for individual Conservation Areas which set out the reasons for designation and an integrated approach to townscape management to co-ordinate public and private investment decisions with a realistic end vision

- implementating proactive enhancement measures which reinforce local character, combining existing resources with potential future funding such as lottery and millenium money. Particular emphasis should be given to environmental improvements to public spaces such as Royal Parks, cemeteries, and churchyards, the reinstatement of railings to London squares, paving, lighting, and street furniture, the restoration of public monuments, and the co-ordinated floodlighting of significant buildings

- co-ordinated planning and design policies for the River Thames to create a high quality environment which acknowledges its historic character, function and visual diversity in Greater London

- recognition of, and protection for, a greater number of strategic and local views of landmark buildings which are crucial to the capital's identity

Implementation of this recommendation would:

- improve the quality of day-to-day decision-making affecting the historic environment.

- highlight the importance of making adequate resources available for effective environmental management

Fig 62 Sicilian Avenue, Camden

• maximise the impact of the historic built environment on London's economy and boost its attraction as a world city

• target particular planning and design matters which need attention

Agencies responsible for implementation:

London Boroughs: Review existing departmental management structures and amend where necessary

English Heritage/LPAC: provide advice on London-wide implications of decisions

Appendix 1: Components of the historic environment

Listed buildings

Designed by the Department of National Heritage, formerly the Department of the Environment. The statutory list of buildings of special architectural or historic interest is drawn up on advice from English Heritage.

Relevant guidance and legislation
DoE Circular 8/87 Historic buildings and Conservation Areas: policy and procedures
Planning (Listed Buildings and Conservation Areas) Act 1990, as amended
Planning (Listed Buildings and Conservation Areas) Regulations 1990
PPG15 Planning and the Historic Environment

Policy objectives
Preservation of features or setting of buildings or structures of special architectural or historic interest.

- Grade I - buildings of exceptional interest

Fig 63 Map of conservation areas

- Grade II* - particularly important buildings of more than special interest

- Grade II - buildings of special interest

'Listed building' can refer to buildings as well as to objects or structures not conventionally described as buildings, for example, bollards, railings, war memorials, boundary walls, pillar boxes, or mile-posts.

Locally listed buildings
Local authorities may prepare non-statutory schedules of locally listed buildings. The local lists may be included in development plans or as an aid when determining boundaries of conservation areas. These may be referred to as buildings of townscape merit, buildings of local interest, or Grade III listed buildings, an obsolete grade.

World Heritage Sites

Designated by statutory list drawn up by inter-governmental World Heritage Committee.

Relevant guidance and legisliation
World Heritage Convention, agreed with UNESCO, ratified in Britain in 1984.

Policy objectives
Identification, protection, conservation, and presentation of cultural and natural sites of outstanding universal value.

No additional national planning restrictions follow from inclusion of site on World Heritage List. However, inclusion is a material consideration. Local planning authorities to include policies regarding World Heritage Sites in development plans.

Conservation Areas

Designated by local planning authority. Conservation Areas may also be designated by the following authorities after consultation with the local planning authority, the Secretary of State, the county planning authority, and in Greater London, English Heritage.

Relevant guidance and legislation
First designated in England under the Civic Amenities Act 1967. Previously planning authorities relied on policies in development plans.
DOE Circular 8/87 *Historic Buildings and Conservation Areas: policy and procedures*
Planning (Listed Buildings and Conservation Areas) Act 1990, as amended
Planning (Listed Buildings and Conservation Areas) Regulations 1990
PPG 15 *Planning and the historic environment*

Policy objectives
Protection and enhancement of the character or appearance of areas which are of demonstrably special architectural or historic interest in a local or regional context. Recently introduced Conservation Area Partnerships enable funds from English Heritage, local authorities, and others to be directed into agreed programmes of work for the preservation and enhancement of Conservation Areas.

The DoE consultation paper *Listed Buildings and Conservation Areas* (1989) proposed greater integration of Conservation Area designation with development plan making process. These proposals were not favourably received and have not been formalised in legislation as yet.

London Squares

Designated by Act of Parliament.

Relevant guidance and legislation
London Squares Preservation Act 1931
Policy objectives
Protection of open spaces in London Squares, as designated under the Act, from over-ground development. Designation does not confer protection of buildings surrounding squares, unless included in a conservation area, or preclude development below ground, eg car parks.

Historic parks and gardens

Designated by English Heritage who maintain the Register of Parks and Gardens of Special Historic Interest in England, a non-statutory definition.

Relevant guidance and legislation
Section 8 of the Historic Buildings and Ancient Monuments Act 1953, as amended by the National Heritage Act 1983, requires English Heritage to notify owners, relevant county and local planning authorities, and the Secretary of State of inclusion and gardens of historic significance.

Policy objectives
To make local planning authorities, prospective developers and other interested parties aware of the presence of parks and gardens of historic significance. Protection is best achieved through inclusion in a conservation area or through specific policies in development plans, as registration does not confer any additional statutory protection.

Fig 64 Map of historic parks and gardens

Heritage land

Proposed by the Countryside Commission and Nature Conservatory Council in 1988, a non-statutory definition.

Relevant guidance and legislation
Heritage Land was not adopted in Strategic Planning Guidance, and was not supported by English Heritage.

Policy objectives
Protection and appropriate management of extensive areas of open land of regional significance for their landscape, historical, and nature conservation interest. Although

Fig 65 Map of heritage land

Heritage Land was not adopted in strategic guidance, some local planning authorities in London have designated areas of Heritage Land on proposals maps and included policies for their protection in Unitary Development Plans. These may or may not have been included in the Heritage Land as previously proposed.

Areas of Special Character

Designated in Greater London Development Plan 1976, a non-statutory definition.

Relevant guidance and legislation
The Greater London Development Plan adopted July 1976 as the Structure Plan for Greater London under the Town and Country Planning Act 1971, as amended by the Town and Country Planning (Amendment) Act 1972.

Policy objectives
The collective preservation of areas contributing to the retention of the character of London as a whole. Designation is hybrid and includes areas of architectural and historical interest, high landscape value, important landmarks or skylines, and the Thames.

This definition is applied inconsistently by the boroughs, including some boroughs who do not use it at all. Many boroughs, while retaining the underlying policy objectives, have changed the name to more closely reflect the issues covered. For example, Bromley designated Areas of Special Character in their old Local Plan which were based on areas identified as Heritage Land by the Countryside Commission and the Nature Conservancy Council. These areas have been replaced with Areas of Special Landscape Character in the Bromley Unitary Development Plan.

Fig 66 Map of areas of special character

Fig 67 Map of strategic views

Strategic views

Designated by the Department of the Environment, on advice from the London Planning Advisory Committee, and included in Unitary Development Plans.

Relevant guidance and legislation
Department of the Environment, 1989 Regional Planning Guidance 3 Strategic guidance for London, London
—, 1991 Final guidance and directions, London
—, 1992 Revised directions, London
—, 1991 Supplementary guidance for London on the protection of strategic views, London

Policy objectives
The protection of views of critical importance to the continuity of London's historic townscape and character.

Areas of Archaeological Priority/Significance

Designation as scheduled by English Heritage under auspices of the Department of National Heritage.

Relevant guidance and legislation
The Ancient Monuments and Archaeological Areas Act, 1979 Planning Policy Guidance note 16 *Archaeology and Planning*

Policy objectives
PPG 16 states that archaeological remains are a 'finite and non-renewable resource, in many cases...vulnerable to damage...'. As such, care is to be taken to ensure that archaeological remains are not destroyed unnecessarily. Their value is noted as sources of knowledge about the past and for their contribution to education, leisure, and tourism.

Many local planning authorities include Areas of Archaeological Priority/Significance/Importance in development plans. Other boroughs prefer a system which involves consultation with English Heritage or the Museum of London on major planning applications likely to impact on archaeological remains.

Scheduled Ancient Monuments

Designated by the Department of National Heritage, formerly Department of the Environment.

Relevant guidance and legislation

The Ancient Monuments and Archaeological Areas Act, 1979

Policy objectives

The protection of monuments of national importance by virtue of their historic, architectural, artistic, or archaeological interest.

Places of worship

Designated by the Department of National Heritage, formerly Department of the Environment.

Relevant guidance and legislation

The Redundant Churches and Other Religious Buildings Act 1969
The Care of Churches and Ecclesiastical Jurisdiction Measure 1991
Pastoral Measure 1983
Planning (Listed Building and Conservation Area) Act 1990

Policy objectives

The preservation of places of worship of special architectural or historical interest. Categories under which churches have been listed were originally separate from the secular listing regime and graded churches as A, B, or C. These grades correspond with Grades I, II*, and II. As English Heritage reviews listed buildings churches are now being regraded using the secular system. Ecclesiastical buildings in use by the Church of England and by denominations with their own internal systems of control are exempt from listed building or conservation area consent.

Fig 68 Map of Areas of Archaeological Priority/Significance

Appendix 2: Major infrastructure projects

Mode	Scheme	Description
Rail	CrossRail	railway in tunnel linking Paddington and Liverpool Street stations through central London
	ThamesLink	
	East London Line extensions	
	Heathrow Express	high-speed rail link from Paddington to existing Heathrow terminals (an extension to the Heathrow Express to serve Terminal 5 is also proposed)
	Channel Tunnel Rail Link	high-speed rail link from the Channel Tunnel to St Pancras
	Woolwich Crossing	extension of the North London Line from the existing terminus at North Woolwich south of the river to Woolwich
Light	Docklands Light Railway(DLR)	extension of the DLR from the existing terminus at Island Gardens River Thames to Lewisham
	Lewisham extension	
	Croydon Light Rail	Light rail system making use of some existing railway lines linking Croydon to Wimbledon in the west and Bromley in the east
Underground	Jubilee Line Extension	extension of the Jubilee Line Underground Line from Green Park to Waterloo, Southwark, and Rotherhithe, then to Canary Wharf and Greenwich Peninsula, terminating at Stratford
	Chelsea-Hackney Line	proposed new underground line linking Chelsea to Hackney, passing through central London
	East London Line extension	proposed extension over existing infrastructure from Shoreditch to Dalston Junction
Road	North Circular (A406) widening	upgrading of the North Circular Road
	Motorway widening	widening of the M3, M4, and M25
	East London River Crossing (ELRC)	second crossing of the River Thames to the east of London
	M11 Link	southern extension to the M11 motorway
	various schemes in the DoT's road programme and Borough programmes	
Air	Terminal 5	construction of a fifth terminal at Heathrow airport and new spur road to the M25
	New heliport	provision of a new heliport facility in central London
	New runway	provision of additional runway capacity in the south-east (a third runway at Heathrow has been ruled out by BAA in the short term)

Appendix 3: Buildings at risk

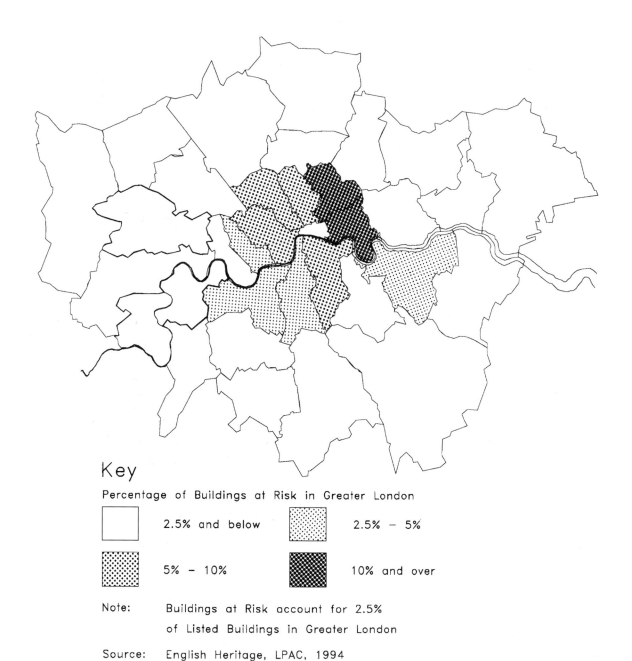

Key

Percentage of Buildings at Risk in Greater London

☐ 2.5% and below	▨ 2.5% – 5%
▨ 5% – 10%	▨ 10% and over

Note: Buildings at Risk account for 2.5% of Listed Buildings in Greater London

Source: English Heritage, LPAC, 1994

Number of Listed Buildings by Borough

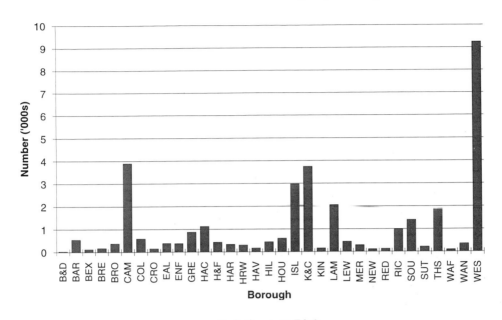

Buildings at Risk

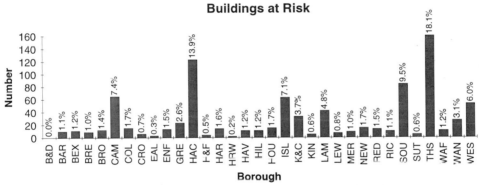

Notes: 1. Buildings at risk are Listed Buildings on English Heritage 'Buildings at Risk' Register
         2. Percentage figures are buildings at risk in each borough as a percentage of the total number of buildings at risk in London

Source: English Heritage, 1994

B&D	Barking & Dagenham	HAC	Hackney	LAM	Lambeth
BAR	Barnet	H&F	Hammersmith & Fulham	LEW	Lewisham
BEX	Bexley	HAR	Haringey	MER	Merton
BRE	Brent	HRW	Harrow	NEW	Newham
BRO	Bromley	HAV	Havering	RED	Redbridge
CAM	Camden	HIL	Hilingdon	RIC	Richmond
COL	City of London	HOU	Hounslow	SOU	Southwark
CRO	Croydon	ISL	Islington	SUT	Sutton
EAL	Ealing	K&C	Kensington & Chelsea	THS	Tower Hamlets
ENF	Enfield			WAF	Waltham Forest
GRE	Greenwich	KIN	Kingston	WAN	Wandsworth
				WES	Westminster

Table 10 Listed buildings and Buildings at Risk

	listed buildings (LB)	Buildings at Risk (BAR)	BAR as % of total London BAR	grade I/A	grade II*/B	grade II/C
Barking & Dagenham	28	0	0.0	0	0	0
Barnet	551	10	1.1	0	0	10
Bexley	123	11	1.2	1	2	8
Brent	175	9	1.0	0	0	9
Bromley	375	12	1.4	0	0	12
Camden	3890	65	7.4	4	1	60
City	590	15	1.7	3	1	11
Croydon	149	6	0.7	0	1	5
Ealing	385	3	0.3	0	1	2
Enfield	378	13	1.5	0	2	11
Greenwich	879	23	2.6	0	5	18
Hackney	1130	123	13.9	2	9	112
Hammersmith & Fulham	434	4	0.5	0	0	4
Haringey	336	14	1.6	0	1	13
Harrow	302	2	0.2	0	0	2
Havering	171	11	1.2	0	0	11
Hillingdon	441	11	1.2	1	1	9
Hounslow	602	15	1.7	0	1	14
Islington	4000*	63	7.1	1	3	59
Kensington & Chelsea	3740	33	3.7	0	6	27
Kingston	156	5	0.6	0	0	5
Lambeth	2063	42	4.8	0	4	38
Lewisham	446	7	0.8	1	0	6
Merton	293	9	1.0	0	1	8
Newham	113	15	1.7	1	1	13
Redbridge	129	13	1.5	0	2	11
Richmond	988	10	1.1	0	2	8
Southwark	1403	84	9.5	0	0	84
Sutton	217	5	0.6	0	0	5
Tower Hamlets	1892	160	18.1	0	5	155
Waltham Forest	100	11	1.2	0	0	11
Wandsworth	352	27	3.1	1	1	25
Westminster	9247	53	6.0	5	1	47
Total/average	35053	844	2.5	20	51	813

Figures for listed buildings refer to entries rather than buildings and were correct as of August 1994.
*An updated list for Islington was published in October 1994 showing an increase in the number of listed buildings in the Borough to approximately 4,000. Source: English Heritage, 1994

Bibliography

Abercrombie, 1943 *County of London Plan*, London

Buchanan, C, 1963 *Traffic in towns*, London

Commission of the European Communities, 1990 *Green paper on the urban environment*, Brussels
Connaughton, J N, 1990 *Real low-energy buildings: the energy challenge*, Plymouth
Countryside Commission, English Heritage, and English Nature, 1993 *Conservation issues in strategic plans*, London

Department of the Environment, 1987 Circular 8/87 *Historic buildings and Conservation Areas*, London
—, 1989a Planning Policy Guidance note 3 *Housing*, London
—, 1989b Regional Planning Guidance 3 *Strategic guidance for London*, London
—, 1990 *This common inheritance - Britain's environmental strategy*, London
—, 1991a Planning Policy Guidance note 17 *Sport and recreation*, London
—, 1991b *Supplementary guidance for London on the protection of strategic views*, London
—, 1992a Planning Policy Guidance note 4 *Industrial development and small firms*, London
—, 1992b Planning Policy Guidance note 12 *Development plans and regional planning guidance*, London
—, 1993 Planning Policy Guidance note 6 *Town centres and major retail development*, London
—, 1994a *Vital and viable town centres: meeting the challenge*, London
—, 1994b *Sustainable development - the UK strategy*, London
—, 1994c Planning Policy Guidance note 15 *Planning and the historic environment*, London

—, 1994d *Ten thousand views of London*, London
—, 1994e Planning Policy Guidance note 13 *Transport*, London
Department of National Heritage, 1993 *Royal Parks Review*, London
Department of National Heritage, English Heritage, and Royal Institution of Chartered Surveyors, 1994 *The listing of buildings: the effect on value*, London

English Heritage, 1984-6 *The Register of parks and gardens of special historic interest*, London
—, 1994 *Register of Buildings at risk in Greater London*, London
—, 1995 *In the public interest: London's civic architecture at risk*, London
English Heritage and Royal Institution of Chartered Surveyors, 1993 *The investment performance of listed buildings*, London
English Historic Towns Forum, 1994 *Traffic in historic town centres*, Bath

Hillman, J, 1991 *Living Cities Report*, London

Jacobs, J, 1961 *The death and life of great American cities*, New York

Local Government Management Board, 1993 *Agenda 21 - a guide for local authorities in the UK*, London
London Planning Advisory Committee, 1991 *Strategic trends and policy, Annual Review*, London
—, 1992a *Issues and choices*, London
—, 1992b *The London office market: assessment and prospects*, London
—, 1993a *London's urban environmental quality*, London
—, 1993b *Industrial land demand in London*, London
—, 1993c *Landscape change in London's Green Belt and metropolitan open land*, London

—, 1994a *Advice on strategic planning guidance for London*, London

—, 1994b *Economic issues working paper: employment change in London 1981-91*, London

—, unpubl *Place and local identity*

London Planning Advisory Committee and London Rivers Association, 1992 *Land-use change and policy on the Thames-side 1967-1991*, London

Naughton, J, 1994 Britain's cities may be dysfunctional planning disasters. But is that any reason to live in the country?, *Observer*, 7 August

Rasmussen, S E, 1934 *London: the unique city*, London

Table 4 Impact of trends on London's historic environment

main changes	key land use implications	effect on the historic environment	examples
population			
fall in the total population of Greater London	pressure on towns beyond the Green Belt	major changes to the historic fabric of towns and villages around London	Reading
	depopulation of inner areas of London	decline of the environment (and services) in inner areas	
transport			
growth in car ownership and usage	new road construction	loss of landmark buildings	
		increased noise, vibration, and pollution	
		severance of communities	
	policies to reduce the impact of the car (traffic calming, pedestrianisation, etc.)	pedestrianisation of historic streets	Deptford High Street
		use of standard materials, surfaces, street furniture, signage, etc	
	introduction of 'red routes'	increased speed and volume of through traffic on designated routes	Upper Street Islington
concentration of transport infrastructure investment to the west of London	motorway construction and the expansion of Heathrow	lack of emphasis on environmental quality and some loss of historic fabric	east and inner London
	development pressure to the west of London		
shift of freight to the roads	release of surplus railway and river-related land/access to rail less important in determining location	industrial dereliction	Kings Cross
investment in public transport infrastructure	redevelopment of transport interchanges	restoration of some historic buildings	Liverpool Street
housing			
change in housing tenure (growth of owner occupation, decrease in rented sector)	demand for new housing units, notably conversions	alteration/sub-division of buildings of architectural/historic merit	London-wide
		on-street parking/use of front gardens for parking	
	reduction in local authority house building and the size of the public housing stock	change in the maintenance of historic estates, streets, etc, reflecting less local authority control	London-wide
reduction in the average household size	demand for new housing units, notably conversions	alteration/sub-division of buildings of architectural/historic merit	London-wide
gentrification	investment in historic properties for residential use	conservation and enhancement of many residental areas	London-wide
London's economy: industry/commerce			
shift from manufacturing to the service sector	increased demand for office space	change of use of historic buildings from industry to services	London-wide particularly in central areas

continued

Table 4 continued

main changes	key land use implications	effect on the historic environment	examples
		major office redevelopment schemes affecting historic sites and changing the skyline and street patterns	Canary Wharf
	reduction in industrial floorspace and land	industrial dereliction	uses along the river Thames
		redevelopment of industrial sites	
amendments to the Use Class Order (eg creation of B1 business class)	over-supply of B1 space	conversion of historic industrial buildings	
	development of mixed-use schemes	new uses introduced to former industrial areas	City fringes
		high vacancy rates in buildings which are not adapted to user requirements	central areas
		'dead' frontages induced by concentrations of financial services, estate agents, etc	
increased bulk carrying and storage of goods	relocation of central markets to outer locations	re-use of old market buildings	Covent Garden, Spitalfields

retail

main changes	key land use implications	effect on the historic environment	examples
growth of large retail outlets	redevelopment of existing town centres	loss of some historic buildings through redevelopment	
		loss of some traditional shop-fronts	
		restoration of some historic buildings	Richmond
		changing street patterns	Kingston
	new out-of-town and edge of centre retail developments	loss of open land	
		re-use of derelict / redundant sites	Hoover Building, Perivale
	trend towards single-use developments	loss of vitality outside day-time hours	
importance of corporate identity	use of similar shop frontages, layouts, signage, etc	standardisation of the high street	

tourism and leisure

main changes	key land use implications	effect on the historic environment	examples
growth of London as a major national and international tourist attraction	provision of tourism infrastructure, including hotels, car parks, etc	loss of land to parking	
		provision of tourism-related facilities and signage in historical areas	Central London
		investment in historic buildings, parks, gardens, etc which secure their future and generate income	
increased participation in sport and leisure activities	provision of new facilities	use of historic parkland for sport (eg golf courses)	
		retention of areas of open space	

continued

Table 4 continued

main changes	key land use implications	effect on the historic environment	examples
reduced church congregations and change from traditional to free evangelical churches	increase in the number of redundant churches	lack of maintenance of churches (and some cemeteries) and exclusion of the general public	London-wide
	change of use of some churches	alterations to historic buildings	

agriculture

intensification of agricultural production in more favoured areas	increase in average field size, removal of hedgerow, etc	degradation of historic landscapes	Ingrebourne Valley, Havering
		erosion of the quality of London's setting	
marginalisation of agricultural production in less favoured areas	incursion of development including mineral extraction, waste disposal, infrastructure, etc	loss of sites and areas of historic importance	Thames Valley to the west of London

technological change

investment in new technology	changes to the urban fabric to accommodate new technology including financial services, security devices, communications, etc	proliferation of facilities in historic sites, and additions to historic buildings	cash dispensers

changes in the public sector/property ownership

changes in the structure of local government in London	strategic planning functions redistributed to the boroughs and various other agencies (eg London Docklands Development Corporation)	planning control over the historic environment split between different agencies	
pressure on local authorities and other public agencies to reduce expenditure	disposal and redevelopment of land and building assets considered surplus to requirements, eg playing fields, schools, hospitals, military establishments, railway land, etc	loss of open space	
		loss/neglect of redundant historic buildings and pressure to redevelop others, leading to blight	Royal Arsenal
restructuring and privatisation of the utilities	disposal and redevelopment of land and buildings assets considered surplus to requirements	loss of open space	Stoke Newington reservoirs
		loss/neglect of redundant historic buildings and pressure to redevelop others, leading to blight	Battersea Power Station
	introduction of competitor services and facilities	proliferation of facilities in historic streets	phone installation for different telecom Companies

growth of the conservation movement

increasing awareness of the value of the historic environment	introduction of conservation legislation	protection of buildings and areas of historic value	London-wide boroughs vary
	incorporation of conservation objectives into land use planning		